YOURTESTIMONIE
SAREWONDERFULT
HEREFOREMYSOUL
KEEPS EXPLORING
THEMTHEENTRANC
EOFYOURWORDSGI
VES PSALMS LIGHT
ITGIVESUNDERST
ANDINGTOTHESIM
PLEIOPENEDMYMO
UTHANDPANTEDFO
RILONGEDFORYOU
RCOMMANDMENTSL
OOKUPON TOM MEAN
DBEMERCIFULTOM
E MANN ASYOURCUS
TOMISTOWARDTHO
SEWHOLOVEYOURN

DEDICATION

This book is dedicated to those who pant for God, to those who hunger and thirst for him, to those who have a distaste for following human thoughts and theologies; to those who are uncomfortable and displeased with all ways except for God's, to those who are searching for what cannot be found on their own but strive to find it nonetheless, to those lovers of God who are seeking for what many people believe is unfindable; and to those who, in spite of all odds and all opposition, crave to peer into the deepest and brightest depths of enlightenment that God has to offer.

CONTENTS

ACKNOWLEDGMENTS

We are not who we are because of ourselves. I must first praise Yahweh and particularly the Holy Spirit for what He has made me to be and for what He has revealed to me. He has also used many human instruments to mold me and this work.

I must thank Robert Schales who first pointed to a glimmer of a light on what I perceived as darkness and uncertainty. His searching for Yahweh has been a light for me. Had he not pointed where to look, I would still be searching.

Armando Sanchez is a dear brother who never wanted to prove a point but always wanted to see God's truth. When he was asked to share his love of God's songs to others, a version of this text was first written. He and his wife Ginger were the first to read this in any form. Had it not been for him, this book would not exist. Although he did not see this little book printed, I hope that I can join him again to sing Praises.

Meladie, my life's partner, has stuck with me through so many things, including my understanding of the Book of Psalms. Even when I made her angry by my not singing man-written songs, she still strove to see what I saw. I remember the day when God illumined her mind. Her joining me has made the journey less lonely.

Most importantly, I must thank those who have misunderstood and challenged me because of my understanding of the Psalms. Without your confrontation, I would not have examined and reexamined the treasures the Holy Spirit has revealed. I would not have had cause to confirm and reconfirm the wonders that God has spread out on a table in front of me. Although they may have meant it for my harm, God has used it to demonstrate His strength through my weakness. The blessings of persecution are too often underrated.

Tom Mann

PREFACE

If anyone plans to read this simple book expecting to learn *everything* there is to know about the Book of Psalms in just a few pages, he will be extremely disappointed. The impetus behind this little work is *not* to explain everything there is to know about this wonderful songbook we call Psalms. That would be impossible. The objectives here are different from most other books about the scriptures.

The first goal is to plant in the reader an appreciation of the songs that should be more alive for us today than they were almost 3000 years ago. Many times the Book of Psalms is viewed much the same way as we view relics behind a glass case in a museum–to be seen but not touched and absolutely never used. To fully appreciate them, we must take them out of the display case, examine them and *use them*.

Second, this book will hopefully give the readers a new perspective so that they can see new things in the Book of Psalms for themselves. Too often we think of learning as memorization of facts. The goal in this book is to allow the readers to see these songs through new eyes: so the readers can gain their own insights and discoveries without memorizing a list from a book–to gain skill and understanding by *using* the songs.

The third goal may be the most difficult, depending on your religious background. Unlike many of the other books of the scriptures, God intended the Book of Psalms to affect us emotionally. It is not a book of facts to be memorized or an exposition on a point of faith: the book was intended to be *felt emotionally and spiritually*. It was intended to make godly feelings well up in us. This fact alone makes it different from the rest of the scriptures. Along with reading, individuals should *sing* the songs. Singing the songs is the best ways to *feel* the songs.

As in the books of prophecy, the Book of Psalms also contains dualities of meaning. Psalm 41 referred to David's close friend who turned on him ("Even my close friend in whom I trusted, Who ate my bread, Has lifted up his heel against me."), and it also applied to Judas in John 13:18 when Jesus poignantly omitted "in whom I trusted." Other songs may have been used by God's people worshipping over 2000 years ago, but the song has real meaning for God's people today.

This little book originally started from a set of lessons written for a friend. There are thirteen chapters that would be suitable for study with a group or a class. Interspersed are several questions intended to provoke the reader's thoughts or to encourage a group discussion. Use these as you see fit. Although "scholars" may find fault with style or tenor or scholastic sources, this book wasn't written for them. This was written for just regular, ordinary Christians.

Each chapter has a song to sing. The lyrics are from public domain sources and may be sung to several, well-known melodies. I apologize that some of the lyrics have outdated language and appear a little stilted. There are modern versions which are copyrighted and could not be legally used here. I'd like to encourage you to drop your inhibitions and "make a joyful noise to the Lord" whenever you can. After all, this is a book about *songs*.

Last, a few Christian denominations sing only songs from the Book of Songs. This practice is generally referred to as "exclusive psalmody." This book does not deal with that subject: such a discussion would be a distraction from this book's objective. However, it is the author's hope that Christians everywhere would gain an appreciation of the Psalms and want to start singing them on their own–as newly found treasures– regardless of their individual understanding or their denomination's creed.

Tom Mann

Not to us, O Lord, not to us,
But to Your name give glory
Because of Your lovingkindness,
Because of Your truth.
    Psalm 115:1

1 : WHAT ARE THE PSALMS

When we approach any study of any book of the scriptures, it is important to know what type of literature or book it is. For example, some are purely history books such as First Chronicles and Second Chronicles. Others are books of prophecy directed to a certain people at a certain time, such as Ezekiel and Isaiah. When we read the books that Paul wrote, we must recognize that they are letters to different groups of Christians, such as Galatians and Ephesians. It is important to know what kind of book we are reading so we can understand it better. When we read the words in the Book of Psalms, we are reading song lyrics.

Read the following song lyrics and then the straightforward sentence below:

Song lyrics:	Straightforward sentence:
Mary had a little lamb, little lamb, little lamb. Mary had a little lamb, its fleece was white as snow.	Mary owned a small lamb that was very white.

Although this example may seem childish, it demonstrates several important differences between how we *sing* and how we *talk*. First, notice that there is a repetition of thoughts and words. We find this in the Book of Psalms, too: phrases and thoughts are repeated to make the thoughts reverberate. Second, there is the use of a metaphor: "its fleece was white *as* snow." Metaphor and simile are the primary tools used throughout the book of Psalms. There is also the use of hyperbole, or exaggeration: even the whitest wool is not quite as "white as snow." On occasion people have taken some of the figures of speech as factual statements and have gotten into theological quagmires.

Repetition is important in understanding something orally. Reading words silently is different from hearing words read aloud. When you read something to yourself, you are able to go back and read passages again. But in reading silently, you also miss the rhythm of the words. When words or phrases are repeated aloud, the listeners tend to remember them better. One reason the Gettysburg address is so powerful is that Abraham Lincoln wrote it with the listeners in mind. Almost all Americans remember the phrase "of the people, by the people and for the people" because of the repetition of the words. So, too, the words in the Book of Psalms were meant primarily to be *heard*. When words are repeated aloud, we tend to remember them. When phrases are repeated in a pattern, we tend to remember them, too. For example, Psalm 136 repeats the phrase "For His lovingkindness is everlasting" twenty-six times. This fact must be very important.

Consider the following passage from Psalm 135. The same phrase is repeated with one component of the sentence being changed each time in a logically progressive order:

O house of Israel, bless the LORD;
O house of Aaron, bless the LORD;
O house of Levi, bless the LORD;
You who revere the LORD, bless the LORD
    Psalm 135:19-20

This type of phrasing and sentence structure makes the phrases easier to remember and to understand.

Reading isn't singing. When we *read* a Psalm, we are not getting the full power of the song. It is like the difference between reading a script for a play and watching a play. The two experiences are completely different: one is reading flat words on a page while the other is seeing actors' expressions and hearing the emotional content of their words. So, when we only *read* a song, we are not getting the full effect. The best way to *experience* a Psalm is to sing it several times over–three times or more. If you can during your study of the Book of Psalms, sing at least one Psalm multiple times so that you memorize it. This way it may become a part of your thoughts. Doing that may help you get a complete experience: how the songs were meant to be experienced.

✓ *If you are using this book as part of a group study, have one person read Psalm 32:8-11 aloud from his or her Bible. Then as a group, sing the song that appears on page 7. What difference did you notice between just reading the words and then singing the words?*

_____

_____

Hebrew songs are different from English songs. We are all used to hearing English poems and song lyrics. We expect to hear words that rhyme and the same feeling or rhythm (meter) when we say the words. The poetry of the ancient world was very different from our modern poetry. The songs in the Book of Psalms have some characteristics that are similar to each other because they are Hebrew poetry. Here are a few of the poetic techniques that are in the Psalms:

Parallelism: Sometimes we see the same idea expressed two times in a row. This is typical of poetry from the ancient middle east. Egyptian and Babylonian poetry from the time period of the Psalms follows the same pattern. What makes this truly amazing is that it allows the poetry to be translated into any language and still retain most of its beauty. Poetry in other languages such as English—which relies on other devices such as rhyming—loses those elements when translated into another language. God had a plan from the start. Sometimes, a Psalm repeats phrases that mean the same thing or uses phrases that are almost the same in meaning, but not quite:

O LORD, who may abide in Your Tent?
Who may dwell on Your holy hill?
    Psalm 15:1

The LORD has heard my supplication,
The LORD receives my prayer.
    Psalm 6:9

The LORD will sustain him upon his sickbed;
In his illness, You restore him to health.
    Psalm 41:3

I will tell of Your name to my brethren;
In the midst of the assembly I will praise You.
    Psalm 22:22

✓ *Read Psalm 25:1-7 aloud:*

> To You, O Lord, I lift up my soul.
> O my God, I trust in You;
> Let me not be ashamed;
> Let not my enemies triumph over me.
> Indeed, let no one who waits on You be ashamed;
> Let those be ashamed who deal treacherously without cause.
> Show me Your ways, O Lord;
> Teach me Your paths.
> Lead me in Your truth and teach me,
> For You *are* the God of my salvation;
> On You I wait all the day.
> Remember, O Lord, Your tender mercies and Your lovingkindnesses,
> For they *are* from of old.
> Do not remember the sins of my youth, nor my transgressions;
> According to Your mercy remember me,
> For Your goodness' sake, O Lord.

How many parallel phrases do you notice?

Metaphors: Metaphors and similes are expressions that compare one thing to another. In *Romeo and Juliet*, Romeo says, "But, soft! what light through yonder window breaks? It is the east, and Juliet is the sun." He does not mean that Juliet is literally the sun, but he is making a comparison between her and the sun.

When Psalm 23 says, "The LORD is my shepherd" it does not literally mean that God is a man who takes care of sheep. It means that God is like a shepherd in many ways. This metaphor is obvious.

David says, "The LORD is my rock" in Psalm 18:2. He is not saying that God is merely a rock or a stone. He is saying that God is solid and immovable like a rock. In Psalm 118, the Psalm says, "That stone is made head cornerstone that builders once despised." This comparison is deeper: we know that "the stone" is Christ and "the builders" are the Jewish leaders of His time and that they would reject the Christ.

Hyperbole: Hyperbole is extreme language that overstates a point for emphasis. For example, sometimes we say, "There is always a line at the checkout." We know that literally there is not *always* a line at the checkout, but we express our feelings that it seems like there is. Jesus used hyperbole when he said, "If anyone comes to me and does not hate his father and mother, his wife and children, his brothers and sisters-yes, even his own life-he cannot be my disciple." (Luke 14:26) Sometimes in the Book of Psalms, a writer uses extreme, exaggerated words to express a strong feeling or emotion.

The following are several examples of hyperbole in the Book of Psalms:

Every night I make my bed swim,
I dissolve my couch with my tears.
       Psalm 6:6

Behold, I was brought forth in iniquity,
And in sin my mother conceived me.
       Psalm 51:5

I hate double-minded people,
But I love your law.
       Psalm 119:113

✓ *When you read the Psalms, look for these techniques as you read and sing. Look back at the Psalm that you sang a couple of minutes ago. Do you see any of these poetic techniques there? If so, what do you see?*

_____

_____

The Psalms are poetry of thoughts, not words. One of the beauties of Hebrew poetry is that it is primarily a poetry of *thoughts*, rather than words. In that way, the *thoughts* can be translated into any language and still maintain most of the power and force that is in the original poem. Because of this, we should not be afraid to use translations of the Book of Psalms. We should also not be afraid of translations or versions of the Psalms that modify the word order but keep the thoughts of the original Psalm. Some Hebrew scholars have noted that the Book of Psalms is more difficult to read than the other Old Testament books because the lines of poetry are just that–poetry. Hebrew poetry is noted for its use of short compact words that do not easily translate. If the Hebrew poems were translated exactly word-for-word, they would usually be nonsense to us in English. For example, read the literal word-for-word translation of Psalm 1:1-2 and then an English translation of the thoughts:

Blessed the man who not has walked the in of counsel the wicked in and of the sinners not has stood and the in of seat scorners not has sat But only the in of the law Jehovah is delight His in and law he meditates day and night *The Interlinear Bible, Hebrew-Greek-English,* Jay P. Green, Sr. General Editor and Translator	Blessed *is* the man Who walks not in the counsel of the ungodly, Nor stands in the path of sinners, Nor sits in the seat of the scornful; But his delight *is* in the law of the LORD, And in His law he meditates day and night. New King James

Did you notice a difference between the two versions? Real translation is not a word-for-word substitution of an English word for a Hebrew word.

Idioms present another problem for translators. An idiom is a phrase that has a meaning other than the literal meaning of the words. An example of an English idiom is "to kick the bucket" which we understand as "to die." When we say, "Joe kicked the bucket" we all know that it means "Joe died" not that "Joe went outside and kicked a bucket." However, other languages do not use this phrase: a strict word-for-word translation from English would be nonsense to non-English speakers. In Hebrew, too, there are these types of phrases where the actual phrases do not convey the meaning when they are translated word-for-word. So a translator must express the *thought* of the words rather than the precise words in their precise order, otherwise the meaning would be meaningless much of the time. When a translator takes those thoughts and allows them to fit into poetry that we understand, without modifying or adding to the inspired thoughts, we get closer to the meaning and emotional content of the original poetry.

✓ *Look back at the lyrics to the psalm on the next page and the Bible version you read aloud at the beginning of this chapter. Were there any differences between lyrics of the two songs? Did any of the phrases of the two songs have different meanings? Sing the song again.*

_____

_____

Psalm 32:8-11

I will instruct thee and thee teach
The way that thou shalt go;
And with mine eye upon thee set,
I will direction show.

Then be not like the horse or mule,
Which do not understand;
Whose mouth, lest they come near to thee,
A bridle must command.

Unto the man that the wicked is
His sorrows shall abound;
But him that trusteth in the Lord
Mercy shall compass round.

Ye righteous, in the Lord be glad,
In Him do ye rejoice;
All ye that upright are in heart,
For joy lift up your voice.

This song can be sung to the following tunes: "America the Beautiful," "How Sweet, How Heavenly," "How Shall the Young Secure Their Hearts," "Jesus, the Very Thought of Thee," "Must Jesus Bear the Cross Alone?" and "When All Thy Mercies."

2 : PSALM
FACTS

Interesting facts about the Book of Psalms. We know that it is a song book. But just what's in it? Who wrote it? The Book of Psalms is in the center of the Bible. It fills a unique niche in the scriptures that no other book does. It is also structured as no other book is. The "chapters" are more properly referred to as "psalms." Here are some facts and trivia:

• It is the longest book in the Bible.
• It also contains the longest "chapter" in the Bible: Psalm 119.
• It also contains the shortest "chapter" in the Bible: Psalm 117.
• Psalm 118 is in the exact center of our arrangement of the scriptures– there are 594 chapters before and after it.
• Psalm 119 is unique in that it has 23 sections, one for each letter of the Hebrew alphabet; each line of that section starts with that letter in Hebrew.
• Children growing up in Israel before Christ would memorize all of Psalm 119.
• During the middle ages, Roman Catholic men were required to memorize the entire Book of Psalms before they could become priests.
• The Book of Psalms was originally divided into five "books": Book One (Psalms 1-41), Book Two (Psalms 42-72), Book Three (Psalms 73-89), Book Four (Psalms 90-106), and Book Five (Psalms 107-150).
• The first four books end in a short "doxology," or special praise to God. The last song in Book Five is entirely a praise.
• Psalms is the most quoted Old Testament book in the New Testament.
• Some people believe the translators of the King James Version (KJV) sneaked in a reference to Shakespeare. The KJV was in the final edit stages in 1610, when Shakespeare was 46. The 46th word from the beginning of Psalm 46 is the word "shake." The 46th word from the end of the psalm is "spear."

• The Bible of the Greek Orthodox Church contains 151 psalms. Psalm 151 is a song celebrating David's defeat over Goliath.
• The Hebrew word *selah* appears repeatedly in the Book of Psalms, and no one knows what it means. The word appears to be an instruction to the singers or musicians.
• The Book of Psalms was the first book printed in the Americas in 1640 in Cambridge, Massachusetts by Stephen Daye.
• Jesus quoted from two psalms as He was dying on the cross: Psalm 22 and Psalm 31.
• There are two numberings of the Psalms, both containing 150 songs. The Hebrew Masoretic text is the basis for most translations. The Septuagint combined several psalms and split several psalms. A few English translations use the Septuagint's numbering, such as the Douay-Rheims.

✓ Sing Psalm 32:8-11 again which is on the last page of this chapter, page 13.

The book has had several names. Sometimes we forget that the names we have now for the books of the Bible are not what they have been called in years past. Even the Bible wasn't called the Bible. The original name for the Book of Psalms was apparently *Prayers*. (See Psalm 72:20.) Then, later, the name of the book in Hebrew was *tehellim* (meaning "praises"): the book got that name because most of the songs are praises to God. Our word "hymn" means "a song of praise to God," so in English it wouldn't be wrong to call the book either "Praises" or "Hymns." However, the name we use now comes from the Greek name for some of the songs in the Book of Praises, *psalmos*. Hundreds of years after the Old Testament was completed, men translated the Hebrew scriptures into Greek in a version call the "Septuagint." Many of our names come from when the Old Testament was translated from Hebrew into Greek. These translators changed the names of many of the books from their old Hebrew names into Greek names: so *Prayers* or *Praises* or *Hymns* became *Psalms*. The term "psalm" comes from the Greek word for plucking a harp and later came to be known for the songs that were sung with a harp and then for just the songs themselves.[1] So, although we now call it the *Book of Psalms*, the Jews called it the *Book of Praises* or *the Book of Hymns*. The Jews of the first century, who spoke Greek (which was a great number of them), would have known the book both by its Hebrew name, *Praises* or *Hymns*, and its Greek name, *Psalms*.

---

[1] The derivation or etymology of a word can easily be confused with its definition. The two are entirely different. The definition or meaning of a word is determined by its usage. For example, the English word *cloak*, a loose overcoat, comes from the French word for *bell*: but we know from usage that no one would "ring a cloak."

✓ *How many names has the Book of Psalms been known by? List the names below:*

_____

_____

What kinds of songs are in the Book of Psalms? The different names for the Book of Psalms gives a clue about its contents. Most of the songs have titles, descriptions, and comments that have been passed down through the centuries and are considered to be reliable. By the century before Christ, they were always included as part of the book. For example, the title for Psalm 51 says that it was written by David when Nathan the prophet came to him, after he had gone in to Bathsheba: the song seems to fit those facts. In the Hebrew, the titles describe the individual songs with the following terms: *prayer, psalm, song, mikhtam, maskil, shiggaion,* and *wedding song.*[2]

The names for the types of songs appear to be interchangeable for the most part. Everyone has seen a Volkswagen Beetle. It holds the record for being the longest and most produced of any model of an automobile. But what was its name? It can be called generically an automobile. Many people called it a "Bug." The Beetle became such a popular model that it was just referred to as "a Volkswagen" even though the company produced other models. The "Beetle" nickname became so popular VW adopted it in the U.S. But the car's real name was the "Type 1." So is it wrong to call a "Type 1" just by the term "Beetle"? If we refer to it as a "car" or an "automobile" rather than a "Volkswagen," no one gets confused or upset. It is that way with the names for most of the songs in the Book of Psalms.

All the "psalms" in the Book of Psalms are "songs." Psalm 45 is described as "A song of love." Psalm 18 is referred to as "a psalm of David...who spoke the words of this song...." Many other songs are identified with both terms. Psalm 86 is just identified plainly as "a prayer"; but when we examine Psalm 70 and Psalm 143–both identified as "a psalm of David"– we see that they are, in fact, prayers to God: "Hear my prayer, O LORD...." Psalm 143:1. So where do the "praises" or "hymns" show up? They are everywhere in the book. Almost every song in the book shouts with praise to God. It is no wonder that the Hebrews called the entire book *Praises.*

---

[2] No one is quite sure what *mikhtams, maskils* and *shiggaion* are. A *maskil* appears to be a term for a "skillful psalm."

So a psalm is a song. A psalm can be a prayer. A song can be a hymn. A psalm can be a praise. Many people struggle with terms and labels: which song is a song, or a psalm, or a prayer, or a hymn, or a praise. These are distinctions between terms that the Holy Spirit did not make. They are struggling with false distinctions that do not make a difference. They have "a morbid interest in...disputes about words...." 1 Timothy 6:4. Or worse, they have no interest at all.

✓ *What names are used for the songs in the Book of Psalms?*

_____

_____

Several different people wrote the Book of Psalms. The Holy Spirit used a number of men to write the songs. Most appear to have been written about the time of the David's and Solomon's reigns. But some were written following the return from exile. The following is a list of writers: the number in parenthesis after the names below indicates the number of songs attributed to that writer.

- *David (73)*: David refers to himself, by inspiration of the Holy Spirit, as the "sweet psalmist of Israel" and that "the Spirit of the LORD spoke by me, And his words were on my tongue." 2 Samuel 23:1-2. David wrote the largest number of songs: often the Book of Psalms is referred to as the "Psalms of David." They may also be referred to as the Psalms of David because David commissioned and organized the use of songs when he designed the temple worship. Jesus referred to David's Psalm 110 as being inspired in Matthew 22:43 and Mark 12:26. Jesus confirms that Psalm 32 was written by David. Peter said David wrote Psalm 2. Acts 4.
- *Asaph (12)*: Asaph was one of David's chief musicians. He was a Levite. Chronicles 15. Jesus referred to Asaph as a prophet. Matthew 13:35.
- *Ethan and Heman (1 each)*: Psalm 89 is attributed to Ethan the Ezrahite. Heman the Ezrahite wrote Psalm 88. In 1 Kings 4:31, Solomon was referred to as being even wiser than Ethan and others; so, Ethan the Ezrahite must have been among a group of very wise men.
- *Solomon (2)*: We know that Solomon was inspired by the Spirit. Psalm 72 and 127 were written by Solomon. Psalm 72 appears quite egotistical if read in the context that he refers to himself; however, it is clear to us today that the song refers to Christ's reign. "May his reign endure forever more...."
- *Moses(1)*: One song is attributed to Moses: Psalm 90.
- *The Sons of Korah (10)*: Korah led a rebellion against Moses in the wilderness. "The line of Korah, however, did not die out." Numbers

26:11. The "sons of Korah" and wrote many of the songs. Their participation in God's great work demonstrates His mercy and love.
• *Anonymous (50)*: Some psalms do not indicate who wrote them.

The Holy Spirit wrote the Book of Psalms. When it all comes down to it, the Holy Spirit wrote the book, and the book is, therefore, authoritative. Jesus referred to them on equal footing with the law and the prophets: "These are My words which I spoke to you while I was still with you, that all things which are written about Me in the Law of Moses and the Prophets and the Psalms must be fulfilled." Luke 24:44. Jesus referred to the Psalms as "law," scripture that cannot be broken. John 10:31-39. Even Satan recognizes the Book of Psalms as authoritative when he quotes from Psalm 91 to tempt Jesus: "If You are the Son of God, throw Yourself down from here; for it is written, 'He will give His angels charge concerning You to guard You,' and 'On their hand they will bear You up, Lest You strike Your foot against a stone.'" Luke 4:9-11. David says that he wrote the songs by the Holy Spirit: "The Spirit of the LORD spoke by me, And his word was on my tongue." 2 Samuel 23:2. Further, many of the "anonymous" psalms are quoted as authoritative in the New Testament:

• Psalm 84 is attributed to Asaph, but Christ said it came from God, has the effect of law and cannot be broken. John 10:31-39.
• The writer of Hebrews quotes from Psalms 2, 95, 97, 102, and 104 as authoritative: he specifically says that the Holy Spirit wrote Psalm 95. Hebrews 3:7-11.
• Psalm 118 is "anonymous," but Jesus quotes it for authority and the Hebrew writer says that God wrote it. Matthew 21:42 and Hebrews 5:6.
• Peter says that David wrote the "anonymous" Psalm 2. Acts 4:25-26
• Paul quotes Psalm 117 as authority. Romans 15:11.
• Satan quotes Psalm 91 as authoritative when he tempted Jesus. Luke 4:10.
• There is a reference in 1 Chronicles 25:1-8 regarding the organization of the "singing to the LORD." The sons of Asaph, Heman and Jeduthun *prophesied* under the direction of Asaph and under the direction of David.

✓ *C. S. Lewis referred to some of the Holy Spirit's Psalms as "vulgar," "petty," "self-righteous," "contemptible" and "devilish." Since the Psalms are inspired by God, are those appropriate words to describe God's work? If we have such a view, is the problem with the inspired songs or with us?*

Why did God choose songs? God made us with a special ability to learn songs and learn by singing. When we were children, our teachers would often teach us songs so that we could learn things easily. Did you learn the letters of the alphabet by learning a song? Did you learn the states of the United States by learning a song? Scientists say that people can remember a song almost word-for-word after having heard it only three times. Sometimes, a song gets stuck in your head so that you can't get it out. The Germans have a term for this: *ohrwurm*. In English it is called an "earworm" or "stuck song syndrome." When God gave his people His songs, He gave them a way to have His words imbedded into their minds. He gave them a way to get His words "stuck" in their hearts. "I will put my law in their minds and write it on their hearts." Jeremiah 31:33

✓ *Here is a challenge. If you are studying with a group, you have sung the song below several times. How much can you repeat from memory?*

Psalm 32:8-11

> I will instruct thee and thee teach
> The way that thou shalt go;
> And with mine eye upon thee set,
> I will direction show.
>
> Then be not like the horse or mule,
> Which do not understand;
> Whose mouth, lest they come near to thee,
> A bridle must command.
>
> Unto the man that the wicked is
> His sorrows shall abound;
> But him that trusteth in the Lord
> Mercy shall compass round.
>
> Ye righteous, in the Lord be glad,
> In Him do ye rejoice;
> All ye that upright are in heart,
> For joy lift up your voice.

This song can be sung to the following tunes: "America the Beautiful," "How Sweet, How Heavenly," "How Shall the Young Secure Their Hearts," "Jesus, the Very Thought of Thee," "Must Jesus Bear the Cross Alone?" and "When All Thy Mercies."

3: PSALMS IN OLD TESTAMENT WORSHIP

Many people consider the Book of Psalms as part of the Law of Moses. In part, it makes sense that one might be led to that conclusion: the book is right in the middle of the Old Testament. Just how did the songs in the Book of Psalms fit into the worship of ancient Israel? In this chapter looks at songs and their use by Israel.

There are more songs in the Bible than just in the Book of Psalms. Just because there is a songbook smack dab in the middle of our Bibles does not mean that other songs are not recorded there. The songs of many people are recorded in the Old Testament. However, these songs were not incorporated into God's songbook, but they were preserved as part of the *history* of Israel. Several examples of these are below:

- Moses's victory song: Moses and the sons of Israel sang a song following God's defeat of the Egyptian army after the crossing of the Red Sea. Exodus 15:1-18
- Miriam's song: Moses's sister, Miriam, is identified as a prophet. She led the women while singing with tambourines and dancing. Exodus 15:21
- The song at Beer: When God gave the Israelites water in the desert at Beer, the Israelites sang a praise to God. Numbers 21:17-18
- Deborah and Barak's song: Following the defeat of Jabin, king of Canaan, Deborah and Barak sang a song praising God for the victory He gave them. Judges 5
- Hannah's song: When God blessed Hannah with a son, she sang a song. 1 Samuel 2

- Goliath's defeat: The women of Israel celebrated the defeat of Goliath, attributing more glory to David than to Saul. Saul was grieved because of this song. 1 Samuel 18:6-8
- David's Song of Deliverance: A song that David wrote celebrating his deliverance. 1 Samuel 22. This song is substantially the same as Psalm 18.
- David's song of thanks for bringing the Ark to Jerusalem: David brought the Ark of the Covenant to Jerusalem with celebration and thanksgiving. Either David or Asaph wrote a song of thanks that is recorded there. Various lines of this song–or at least the thoughts–appear throughout the Book of Psalms. 1 Chronicles 16
- Jeremiah's song regarding the remnant: Through Jeremiah, God said that the Israelites of that time should sing this song following their deliverance from captivity. Jeremiah 31:7-9

√ *How are these songs similar? How are they different from the songs in the Book of Psalms?*

_____

_____

There was only one song under the Law of Moses. The Law of Moses is contained in the books of Exodus, Leviticus, Numbers and Deuteronomy. God's law for the new nation of Israel was vast in its scope and meticulous in its detail. There has been nothing like it given to any people until Christ. Detailed requirements aside, there was almost no use of music under the Law of Moses. If an Israelite were to have kept the law perfectly (which was not done except by Christ), he or she would only have had to sing one song!

There was some "music" commanded by Moses. In Numbers 10, God instructed the priests to blow trumpets as part of a feast celebration. There is no indication that this was a specific melody: rather it was a blast of trumpets that was to call the people together, to remind them that God would come to their aid in time of battle, and to announce the beginning of the festivals or feasts. The trumpets were made of hammered silver and were only to be blown by the priests. In Numbers 29, God established what has been called "The Feast of the Trumpets." Apparently, there were seven trumpets. 1 Chronicles 15:24.

Nevertheless, there was still only one song. Moses recounted the law to the generation of Israelites that was to enter into Canaan and to take possession of the promised land. Just before Moses died, God, through

Moses, wrote a song to be a witness for God and to remind Israel what God had done for them. "So Moses wrote this song the same day, and taught it to the sons of Israel." Deuteronomy 31:14-22. Moses then spoke the words of the song in the hearing of all the assembly of Israel. The lyrics are contained in Deuteronomy 32:1-43. God told them to sing it and teach the song to their children.

✓ *Read the Song of Moses, Deuteronomy 32:1-43. If you are using this book as part of a group study, you may wish to read a short section of it. Why do you think it was important for the Israelites to know this song? Why do you think God put this message into a song?*

David designed musical worship for the Temple. David was a musician at his core. He was very skillful at playing the harp. 1 Samuel 16:18. When King Saul needed calming music, David was brought in to play his harp for the king, and the terrorizing spirit would depart from Saul. When David became king of Israel, he wanted to build the Temple as a permanent home for the Ark of the Covenant. Although God prohibited David from building the Temple, David did everything except build it. He assembled the materials for the Temple and prepared the plans for the temple and its furnishings. 1 Chronicles 28. He even wrote the song, Psalm 30, that was to be used upon the dedication of the Temple after his death. David also wrote, organized, and designed the worship for the Temple, including musical accompaniment and songs. When Temple worship was restored, the practices were described:

> And they kept the charge of their God, and the charge of the purification, and so did the singers and the porters, according to the commandment of David, and of Solomon his son. For in the days of David and Asaph of old there was a chief of the singers, and songs of praise and thanksgiving unto God.
> Nehemiah 12:45-46.

The distinction between the Law of Moses and the Ordinance of David is brought out in 2 Chronicles 23:18 when Joash restored the Temple worship that had been long forgotten: Jehoiada set up the Levitical priests "to offer burnt offerings of the LORD, as it is written in the law of Moses–with rejoicing and singing according to the order of David." The Law of Moses and the Order of David are completely separate things

✓ David was "a man after God's own heart." Acts 13:22. No other person in scripture is described this way.[3] How does this fact influence your reading or singing of the Psalms, the songs he wrote and commissioned?

_____

_____

The Psalms Sprang from a New Tabernacle. There was a time in the history of Israel when the Ark of the Covenant became separated from the Tabernacle of Moses. The Tabernacle of Moses was at Gibeon, which was about ten miles from Jerusalem. David was prohibited from approaching it. 1 Chronicles 21. The Tabernacle of Moses became a place of ritualistic sacrifice. However, God was not there: the Holy of Holies was empty. Where was the Ark of the Covenant? Saul and Eli had tried to use the Ark as a sort of "secret weapon" when they battled with the Philistines: it didn't work. When the ark finally returned to Israel it was not returned to the Tabernacle. It was placed in the house of Obed-Edom, the Gittite. 2 Samuel 6:10-12. At that time David prepared a second tabernacle on Mount Zion, which became known as David's Tabernacle. 2 Samuel 6:17, Isaiah 16:5, Amos 9:11, and Acts 15:16. Moses's Tabernacle was silent. David's Tabernacle became a place where people could see the Ark and it became a place of celebration–a place of song!

The first use of song in association with the worship of God (other than Moses's song in Exodus 32) is when David brought the Ark of the Covenant to Jerusalem. 1 Chronicles 15:27. In preparation for this event, David "spoke to the chiefs of the Levites to appoint their relatives as the singers, with instruments of music, harps, lyres, loud-sounding cymbals, to raise sounds of joy." They appointed Asaph, Heman and Ethan in charge of the music.[4] 1 Chronicles 15:16-17. David had prepared for this event with meticulous detail in advance. He had clothes made for himself, had arranged order of the procession and wrote special music for the event. David dressed in linen and an ephod, which was an elaborate outer garment used mostly by priests. The Ark of the Covenant was brought to Jerusalem with great fanfare: singing, dancing, and loud sounding of cymbals and horns. There were seven men sounding horns and three men sounding cymbals, each leading a procession of men

_____

[3] Because Jesus is God, His heart isn't _like_ God's. His heart _is_ God's. "If you have seen Me, you have seen the Father." John 14:9.

[4] These three men are specifically identified as having written a number of songs among them.

behind them. Once the Ark was placed in his Tabernacle, David arranged for Asaph to sing a song that had already been written and practiced.

Once the Ark was brought to David's Tabernacle, music immediately became a regular part of the service to God by the Levites. Specifically, Heman and Jeduthun were designated "to give thanks to the LORD, because his lovingkindness is everlasting."[5] This practice of giving thanks for God's grace continued daily, with trumpets, cymbals and loud songs by a professional group of singers chosen from the Levites. 1 Chronicles 16:41-42.

More than just a quirky historical even, David's Tabernacle was a foreshadowing of the relationship we have through Christ.[6] It was an amazing time in the Nation of Israel:

> God's people are worshipping freely. They are singing without fail. They are full of joy. There is life. There is glory. But even more thrilling, the ark is in full view of the people. There's no veil to close it off. God's holy presence is open for all to enjoy—not just the priests....While the priests are slinging blood over at the Tabernacle of Moses in Gibeon, there are no blood sacrifices in Zion. David offered only one sacrifice when he brought the ark to Jerusalem. This represents the fact that, in Zion, the people of God are not conscious of their sins....Worship at the tabernacle of David went on twenty-four hours a day, on the hour, for forty years. "Praise the LORD, all you servants of the LORD who minister by night in the house of the LORD" (Ps. 134:1). This psalm is a reference to the night shift. God's people worshipped, sang, and praised their Lord around the clock in the tabernacle of David. It's the most amazing scene in all the Old Testament. And as unbelievable as it sounds, it was the new covenant experience right smack dab in the Old Testament era.[7]

It was precisely in this unique period in the history of Israel, that God gave us the Psalms. Initially, they were completely independent of the Law of Moses and the sacrifices. God gave us the Psalms during a "new covenant experience" of worship that was detached from the Law of Moses–literally miles removed from the symbolic sacrifices–but overflowing with pictures of the fulfillment and reality to come.

---

[5] It is likely that Psalm 136 was used in this occasion because every other line repeats this exact phrase, and the song refers only to events prior to David's rule.

[6] See Amos 9:11-12 and Acts 15:16.

[7] Frank Viola, *From Eternity to Here,* 150-151.

The Psalms become an overlay of Temple worship. After this great event, music was a permanent, integral part of the Levite's practice in Temple worship. The use of music, and the Psalms in particular, did not change the basic worship under the Law of Moses. Instead, they added an extra element to it. An entire group of trained singers from the tribe of Levi were dedicated to this service. Twenty-four divisions served in rotation in continuous song. 1 Chronicles 25.

Music became associated with each day, each sacrifice and each festival. They were used for entrance ceremonies and processions by the Levites and as accompaniment by pilgrims on trips to worship. The Israelites also used the songs collectively in times of distress and in times of joy. In the Temple, specific Psalms came to be used at all the sacrifices and ceremonies. A different Psalm was assigned to start each day of the week. According to the Septuagint and the Mishna,[8] each day of the week had its own special song:

Sunday	Monday	Tuesday	Wednesday	Thursday	Friday	Saturday
Psalm 24	Psalm 48	Psalm 82	Psalm 94	Psalm 81	Psalm 93	Psalm 92

At the beginning of the day when the high priest poured the libation of wine on the altar, the chief musician would sound the cymbals and the singers would sing that day's song. The song traditionally was sung in three sections: between each section the singers would be silent and the priests would sound the silver trumpets. At the signal of the trumpets, the worshippers bowed down before the altar. Similar practices continued throughout the day depending on that day's rituals.

Exactly which songs were used with which ritual is not illuminated in the scriptures and have been lost through time. From tradition and from the content of some of the songs, we can get a good idea of the uses of several songs:

- *Feast of the Tabernacles:* Psalm 81
- *Passover:* Psalms 113 and 114 were traditionally sung by families before the Passover meal. After the Passover meal, the family would sing Psalms 115-118. Most authorities believe that the latter group of songs were sung by Christ and the disciples after the Passover feast in Mark 14:26.
- *Ascending to Jerusalem on a pilgrimage:* Psalms 120-134 are labeled as "Songs of Ascent." Most believe that they were sung by Israelites as

[8] The Mishna is a written version of the oral traditions of the Jews dating from about 220 A.D.

they traveled up to Jerusalem to worship. "You will have songs as in the night when you keep the festival; and gladness of heart as when one marches to the sound of the flute, to go to the mountain of the LORD, to the Rock of Israel." Isaiah 30:29. The lyrics of these songs seem to be suitable as accompaniment for a trip to Jerusalem.

- *A Morning Prayer:* Psalm 3 is identified as "Morning Prayer of Trust in God." The song states, "I lay down and slept; I awoke for the LORD sustains me."
- *An Evening Prayer:* Psalm 4 is labeled as an evening prayer. "In peace I will both lie down and sleep, for You alone, O LORD, make me to dwell in safety." God gave us such great words to sing as we lie down to sleep.

√ *If you are studying this book as part of a group, sing Psalm 117 below. The tune is one we commonly know as "Joy to the World." (Optionally, you may sing it with any of the tunes listed in Chapter 2 without the last line repeated.)*

> O all ye nations of the earth,
> Praise ye the mighty Lord;
> And all ye people magnify
> His name with one accord,
> His name with one accord,
> His name with one accord.
>
> For great to us his mercies are,
> And loving kindnesses;
> His truth endures for evermore
> The Lord O do ye bless,
> The Lord O do ye bless,
> The Lord O do ye bless.

√ *The term for "grace" that we are familiar with in the New Testament appears as "lovingkindness" in the Book of Psalms. Consider this song in conjunction with Christ's trial and crucifixion. How does this song relate to Christ's sacrifice?*

_____

_____

4 : PSALMS AFTER SOLOMON

If you ever have the opportunity to view the Crown Jewels of England, you may be amazed and possibly a little disappointed. Some of the crowns that graced the heads of monarchs are skillfully crafted with incomparable beauty. However, they have no jewels in them. The jewels were taken from one crown and then inset on a new crown for a new monarch. Some jewels have been left separate and sparkle all by themselves. In a similar way, the jewels of the scripture–the Psalms–have had multiple uses throughout history. They moved from Temple to exile into homes and to synagogues and then to the early church.

The musical score plus the director's commentary. Have you ever seen a silent movie with no background music? It still has the same meaning and story, but it is missing the depth and drama music provides. The singing of the songs from the Book of Psalms supplemented the Temple worship, providing an extra dimension to the rituals. The music didn't change the rituals, but it enhanced them. The music punctuated the various acts with the words enhancing the actions of the priest. Some DVD's of Hollywood movies contain optional running commentaries you can hear while watching the films. The director of the movie describes the action, or he tells you what he was thinking when he filmed a particular scene. He might point out something in this scene that sets up another scene later on. Although you might enjoy a movie just watching it without the commentary, you have a deeper understanding of the movie knowing what was going on behind the scenes. That is sort of what God provided with the Book of Psalms. The Holy Spirit's lyrics enhanced and explained the actions and the rituals. The lyrics make connections between events and rituals. They highlight what God views as important.

✓ *Read about the Feast of the Tabernacles in Leviticus 23:34-36 and 39-44. Now read Psalm 81. If you were an Israelite celebrating this feast, how would this song help you understand the feast more clearly?*

The lyrics of the songs are a running commentary on the *symbols* of the Old Covenant. The meanings of symbols in the song lyrics were veiled–not understandable–to the original hearers. 2 Corinthians 3:12-16. The meanings of the Psalms are still veiled today to those who do not view the Psalms through Christ. We know from the New Testament that the Law of Moses was a foreshadowing of what was to come under Christ. Hebrews 9. We know that the Temple is the Church and individual Christians are "living stones." 1 Peter 2:4-5. The Levitical priesthood has been replaced: Christ is now the High Priest, and we are priests. Hebrews 9:11-12 and 1 Peter 2:9. We know that the animal sacrifices for atonement are figures and representation of the sacrifice of Jesus on the cross. John 1:29. Jerusalem also represents the church. Galatians 4:21-31. The list could go on and on. The inspired songs illuminated the sacrifices and rituals at the very instant they occurred. How amazing that must have been to see the priestly rituals and to hear the songs.

✓ *Read Isaiah 60:6 and Matthew 2:10-11 Then read Psalm 72:12-19. To whom is this referring? Why do you think so?*

The connections are cut. God did not preserve the connections between the songs He wrote and the sacrifices and rituals He commanded. He cut those links: "...whatever these ceremonies were, they have receded so far into the background that they are virtually impossible to recover from the psalms in their present form."[9] If we knew which song was used with which sacrifice, our view of that song would be limited and narrow. God has hidden the song-ritual connection; therefore, the Psalms have a universal appeal because we can see them in the larger context of God's entire plan for us through Christ. For example, although many of the songs were written as a result of an attack by a particular enemy, such as Saul, Absalom, or the Philistines, the Holy Spirit never refers to the

---

[9] Philip R. Davies and John William Rogerson, *The Old Testament World,* 158.

enemy by name: He refers to "my enemies" or "my foes." When viewed through the telescope of history, we see now that the Holy Spirit is referring to Satan and the enemies of God and the enemies of His people.

The Babylonian captivity changed the way the songs were used. When Judah was taken into captivity, the Temple fell silent. The Babylonians captured the priests and stole the instruments of music. However, music did not stop; the music flourished. The inspired men of the day added songs regarding captivity and then later about restoration. The music fundamentally changed in a way that affects us even today.

Although their access to the Temple was cut off, the Jews remembered the songs of the Temple. They could not all carry the Law of Moses in their satchels, but they could carry the Psalms of God in their hearts. They could sing the songs in their houses and while they were working. The songs were easily passed on to their children. Additionally, the exiles turned to studying the Law of Moses in small groups, synagogues, in all the communities where they had been sent. There were not necessarily priests–much less musically trained priests–in every community. The main purpose of the synagogue was for studying the law, and naturally, the inspired songs were an essential aspect of synagogue worship. Without trained musicians, the Psalms were sung without musical accompaniment, or *a capella*.[10] Divorced from ritual, the Psalms gained greater power in the lives of God's people:

> The synagogue had no altar; therefore no sacrifices could be performed there. As the people had learned in Babylon, the psalms lost none of their spiritual power by being sung independently of these...Psalm-singing, with its stimulus to the spirit, gradually crept into the service; first mere portions, then entire psalms were added to the [public scripture readings], benedictions, and prayers.[11]

Because ritual and sacrifices were impossible for the dispersed multitude of Jews, the Psalms became their spiritual connection to God, Jerusalem, the Temple and the sacrifices.

---

[10] This practice of singing without instrumental accompaniment continues today in many Christian religious groups: the Amish, most Churches of Christ, the Eastern Orthodox Christian Church, the Old German Baptist Brethren, Old Regular Baptists, and Old Order Mennonites and Conservative Mennonites, Plymouth Brethren, Primitive Baptists, and some Presbyterian churches.

[11] Alfred Sendry and Mildred Norton, *David's Harp*, 222.

The Jews were unified in lyrics and melody. As the Jews were spreading throughout the world, synagogues sprang up in nearly every city in the Greek and then Roman empires. Teaching was the main goal of each synagogue. The main method used for transferring knowledge was chanting psalms. Remember in our first chapter how rhythm and melody help people remember words? The same thing was done in the synagogues: the Psalms were memorized through singing. After the exile when Temple worship began again, the common Jew had a closer connection with the synagogue than with the Temple. So twice a year, one or two leaders of a local synagogue would travel to Jerusalem with the primary goal of learning the proper rituals, songs, and pronunciations to preserve the Jewish traditions throughout the world. So in this way, the singing of the Psalms were preserved, standardizing the practices throughout the world. However, by about 200 B.C. a Greek influence in music crept into the synagogues

The tunes have been lost in time. It is clear from the notes accompanying the songs, that specific melodies were used. For example, the notes to Psalm 9 say it was sung to the tune of "The Death of a Son." Psalm 22 was to the tune of "The Doe of the Morning." Not all tunes were original compositions: contemporary tunes were adapted for religious lyrics. Even today, many modern worship songs use tunes that were originally "secular." So then, just as now, the tunes themselves were not central: the lyrics to the songs were important. You can learn the words to a song faster if you use a familiar tune: you don't have to concentrate on learning two things at once.

✓ *Sing Psalm 117, that was to the tune of "Joy to the World," again now. Did that familiar tune help you learn the lyrics faster than if you had to learn a new tune, also?*

What did the songs sound like? No one knows for sure. But scholars guess that it would most resemble what we would recognize as sounding like modern Middle Eastern music or Muslim calls to prayer. The Semitic world did not use the same tone scale and rhythm that we use today. To our ears the Arab songs seem more like chants than songs. Our musical traditions come from ancient Greece: those ancient notes and rhythms form the foundation of our music today. We would immediately recognize an ancient Greek song as a song: it would have the kind of tune and rhythm we are familiar with. Because synagogues through the world were far from Jerusalem's influence, the Greek musical traditions and tunes came into synagogue worship. The lyrics were the same, but the tunes for the Psalms were slowly being Hellenized–made to sound like Greek songs. This was especially the case in the communities of Jews living in centers of heavy Greek and Roman influence. So by the time of Christ, the songs in the Book of Hymns (in Hebrew) or Book of Psalms (in Greek) were sung everywhere in the known world to both Hebrew and Greek tunes.

✓ *Some religious groups still chant their songs today, adhering to ancient traditions for their "tunes." Do you think that chanting is the best way for us to express Praise or Hymns to God today in our culture? Does culture affect the tunes and songs we use in our worship today?*

✓ *As you did at the end of the last chapter, sing Psalm 117 below. The tune is one we commonly know as "Joy to the World."*

> O all ye nations of the earth,
> Praise ye the mighty Lord;
> And all ye people magnify
> His name with one accord,
> His name with one accord,
> His name with one accord.
>
> For great to us his mercies are,
> And loving kindnesses;
> His truth endures for evermore
> The Lord O do ye bless,
> The Lord O do ye bless,
> The Lord O do ye bless.

This can also be sung without repeating the last line to "America the Beautiful," "How Sweet, How Heavenly," "How Shall the Young Secure Their Hearts," "Jesus, the Very Thought of Thee," "Must Jesus Bear the Cross Alone?," or "When All Thy Mercies."

5:GOD'S SELF TALK FOR US

Fyona Campbell was the first woman to walk around the world. At age 24 she walked the entire length of Africa through deserts and jungles. When someone asked her why she walked over 9,900 African miles, she said, "Because I said I would!" Nearly everyone acknowledges that our words affect our thoughts and our thoughts affect our words. Then, our words and thoughts together become a self-talk that affect our actions. One group of professional career developers noted that in order for self-talk to be effective, it must be (a) in the present tense, (b) in precise language, and (c) repeated often.[12] We find this pattern often in the Book of Psalms. "As a man thinks within himself, so is he." Proverbs 23:7.

Our words from God. God's words to Ourselves. The Book of Psalms is full of songs that contain just this type of self-talk. "As the deer pants for the water brooks, so my soul pants for You, O God. My soul thirsts for God, for the living God..." Psalm 42:1-2. If we don't feel that thirst at first, we learn to feel it when we sing that song to ourselves. Many songs contain statements that are a sort of self-talk, where the singer admonishes, encourages and teaches himself to live a more godly life. When in a group, the singers would have spoken to one another–teaching truths to each other. The importance of this self talk is demonstrated by that attention that God gave to it. The longest song in the book, Psalm 119, is 176 verses of positive self-talk.

---

[12] http://brandonpartners.com/docs/SelfMotivationBk.pdf, retrieved January 29, 2013.

√ *On page 31 are words to Psalm 119:161-168. Sing it now. Notice all the "I" statements in this song.*

√ *Would memorizing this Psalm and singing this Psalm repeatedly change the thinking of the Israelites? How would it change* your *thinking?*

_____

_____

Songs of uprightness, despair and comfort. Probably the most well-known, comforting song is Psalm 23. Even if they are not religious, most people recognize the words even if they don't know where they came from. Although the song is thousands of years old, people still read it aloud and often read it right along with "the Lord's Prayer" at funerals and public occasions. However, the book contains other songs of equal if not greater power, where God gives comfort through this same kind of self talk. Many of these songs present a problem and then a solution. Several psalms deal with human problems and frailty. Unfortunately, because of time limitations, only shorter songs or sections of songs are discussed in this section.

Psalm 63: Expressing Love. This is probably one of the deepest expressions of love for God in the scriptures. Augustine said that one can sing nothing worthy of God except what God has given him. Only God's words can express the deep love we should have for Him.

Psalm 63	Thoughts
O God, You *are* my God; Early will I seek You; My soul thirsts for You; My flesh longs for You In a dry and thirsty land Where there is no water. So I have looked for You in the sanctuary, To see Your power and Your glory.	*What does the singer of this song need?* *Where does he look to find it?*

Psalm 63 (continued)	Thoughts (continued)
Because Your lovingkindness *is* better than life, My lips shall praise You. Thus I will bless You while I live; I will lift up my hands in Your name. My soul shall be satisfied as with marrow and fatness, And my mouth shall praise *You* with joyful lips.	*There is an intimate connection between praise and an aspect of God. What is it and how are they connected?*
When I remember You on my bed, I meditate on You in the *night* watches. Because You have been my help, Therefore in the shadow of Your wings I will rejoice. My soul follows close behind You; Your right hand upholds me.	*Here there is a connection between the past and the singer's actions now. What did God do? What does the singer do now?*
But those *who* seek my life, to destroy *it*, Shall go into the lower parts of the earth. They shall fall by the sword; They shall be a portion for jackals.	*Why are these thoughts comforting? If this is thought of as one's spiritual life rather than physical life, does this make more sense?*
But the king shall rejoice in God; Everyone who swears by Him shall glory; But the mouth of those who speak lies shall be stopped.	*Spiritually, who is the king? Who are those who "swear by Him"? Explain the reference to the liars?*

Psalm 131: A simple, humble heart. This song's lyrics are a precursor to Jesus's statement, "Blessed are the humble...." Matthew 5:5.

Psalm 131	Thoughts
Lord, my heart is not haughty, Nor my eyes lofty. Neither do I concern myself with great matters, Nor with things too profound for me.	*What is the attitude of the singer here?*
Surely I have calmed and quieted my soul, Like a weaned child with his mother; Like a weaned child *is* my soul within me.	*Read Matthew 18:1-4. Do you see a connection? Rather than "weaned child," we would probably say "toddler." How should a follower of God be like a toddler?*
O Israel, hope in the Lord From this time forth and forever.	*Why is Israel mentioned here?*

Psalm 101: Uprightness. Now let us look at the first four verses of Psalm 101. There is a subtle difference between the word *will* and the word *shall.* The word *will* refers to the will of the person speaking and his intentions to do something in the future. The word *shall* refers to the certainty in the future regardless of the person's will.

Psalm 101	Thoughts
I will behave wisely in a perfect way. Oh, when will You come to me? I will walk within my house with a perfect heart. I will set nothing wicked before my eyes; I hate the work of those who fall away; It shall not cling to me. A perverse heart shall depart from me; I will not know wickedness.	*What kind of day would the singer of this song have if he had sung this often?* *How would this song have affected his attitude toward daily life?*

Psalm 27: Courage. John said that perfect love casts out fear. 1 John 4:18. The Surgeon General of the United States reported that over sixteen percent of adults suffer from anxiety disorders directly resulting from fears. Another eight percent suffer from some type of phobia that prohibits them from functioning normally. Together, about one-fourth of the United States has mental conditions related to fear. It is no wonder that God addressed this many times to His people. "I will not be afraid of ten thousands of people who have set themselves against me round about." Psalm 3:6.

Psalm 27:1-3	Thoughts
The Lord *is* my light and my salvation; Whom shall I fear? The Lord *is* the strength of my life; Of whom shall I be afraid? When the wicked came against me To eat up my flesh, My enemies and foes, They stumbled and fell. Though an army may encamp against me, My heart shall not fear; Though war may rise against me, In this I *will be* confident.	*Jesus said, "And do not fear those who kill the body but cannot kill the soul. But rather fear Him who is able to destroy both soul and body in hell." Matthew 10:28. How would this self-talk help someone in distress?*

Psalm 139: Everything and Everywhere. Psalm 139 is a longer song that gives great assurances to the person singing it. Here are some highlights:

Psalm 139	Thoughts
1-2	
O Lord, You have searched me and known me. You know my sitting down and my rising up; You understand my thoughts afar off.	*Is there anything about our activities and thoughts that God does not know?*
7-8	
Where can I go from Your Spirit? Or where can I flee from Your presence? If I ascend into heaven, You *are* there; If I make my bed in hell, behold, You *are* there.	*Is there anywhere we can go where God isn't?*
15-16	
My frame was not hidden from You, When I was made in secret, *And* skillfully wrought in the lowest parts of the earth. Your eyes saw my substance, being yet unformed.	*God knew everything about us even while we were still being formed.*

Lies of Satan. Man's "Truth." God's Truth. The Book of Psalms offers the most powerful way to imbed truth into the hearts of God's people. Satan is the father of lies, and he does everything he can to imprint his lies into our minds. Every person alive has "bought in" to Satan's lies. Our battle in this life is to overcome the lies of Satan with the Truth of God. All humans have replaced the Truth of God for a lie and have been taken captive by Satan's lies. Romans 1:25 and 2 Timothy 2:24-26. Even the best human knowledge and "understanding" of God's ways can't replace God's Truth. The only way to replace Satan's lies is directly from God's Truth revealed in scripture. The Psalms stamp those truths directly into the singers' hearts.

✓ *Satan's lies are everywhere and only God's truth can overcome these lies. Are human thoughts or words powerful or authoritative enough to overcome Satan's lies?*

✓ *If you are studying this book with a group, sing Psalm 119:161-168 again, which appears below.*

✓ *Here is a challenge for you. Sing this song once or twice a day, every day this coming week–perhaps every morning and evening. At the end of the week, see if you notice any change in how you lived.*

Psalm 119:161-168

Princes have persecuted me,
Although no cause they saw:
But still of thy most holy word
My heart doth stand in awe.

I at thy word rejoice, as one
Of spoil that finds great store.
Thy law I love; but lying all
I hate and do abhor.

Sev'n times a-day it is my care
To give due praise to thee;
Because of all thy judgments, Lord,
Which righteous ever be.

Great peace have they who love thy law;
Offense they shall have none.
I hop'd for thy salvation, Lord,
And thy commands have done.

My soul thy testimonies pure
Observed carefully;
On them my heart is set, and them
I love exceedingly.

Thy testimonies and thy laws
I kept with special care;
For all my works and ways each one
Before thee open are.

This may be sung to the tune of "Amazing Grace" or any of the tunes used previously.

6:SHADOWS COME TO LIFE

Wayang Kulit is a storytelling form in Indonesia that is over a thousand years old. Elaborate flat puppets are painted in bright colors, very similar to jointed paper dolls. The puppeteers manipulate the figures from behind a white sheet with a bright light casting a shadow on the sheet allowing the audience to see the performance. Although the puppets themselves are very detailed and colorful, the audience only sees shadows and outlines. The performance of the shadows creates a certain mystery around them, powerfully elevating the performances above puppet shows we know in western cultures. Unless the audience were permitted to look behind the curtain at the actual object casting the shadow, they would be ignorant of the puppet's colorful details. At the right is a photo of one of those puppets.[13]

In a similar way, the people living under the Old Testament could only see the shadows of the real things to come under Christ. The Law of Moses was a detailed picture of what was to come, but it was only a shadowy, earthly representation of real spiritual relationships. However, real, spiritual truths were hidden by a veil or curtain, allowing people and

---

[13] This photograph and the drawing on the next page were in the public domain and not subject to the copyright laws of the United States on the date of publication.

angels to get glimpses of shadows of what was to come. Now the things that angels longed to see, the mysteries of old, are revealed through Christ. 1 Peter 1:10-12 and 2 Corinthians 3:12-18.

An artist's drawing of a Jewish high priest.

Some people view the Psalms as just old remnants of a nation that has died and of an old law that has been brushed aside. They cannot see–or refuse to see–anything but impotent shadows. In reality, the Psalms are very much alive when viewed from this side of the screen or veil. Instead of seeing merely the shadows in the Psalms, we can see the very living, active spiritual things of God. And we can see the living Christ. This chapter examines some of the images of Christ.

✓ On the page 38 are the words to a part of Psalm 89. Stop and sing the song now.

Mrs. Middleton in a grocery store. When you were a kindergartener (or first or second grader for that matter), did you ever run into your teacher at the grocery store? Most children are shocked to learn that their teacher who they love and is the center of their lives for most of the day, actually exists and does things outside of the classroom. When her son or daughter visits her one day and calls her "Mom," the students also suffer from shock: how can these strange adults call her anything other than Mrs. Middleton? (My kindergarten teacher was Mrs. Middleton.) And when I overheard my teacher being called by her first name, I was fascinated. Her name can't be "Sarah"! It's Mrs. Middleton! If her husband came to school and called her "honey." or "sugar," we would probably be confused–she's not a jar of sweet stuff! We must have heard wrong. As we mature and if we are fortunate enough to stay in contact with our old teachers, we find out that they have first names, middle names, maiden names, and nicknames. They also have different titles, jobs, volunteer roles, etc.

As Christians today, we first met Jesus in the Gospels. We are used to calling Him "Jesus." But that's not his only name. "Jesus" just happens to be the name used when we first met him and got to know him. He has many other names. Jesus is also known by His "job" titles and "functions." Many young Christians are disoriented at first when they learn that Jesus has more names than just "Jesus" and that they can call Him or refer to Him by any of those names, titles and functions. But as mature Christians, we know that the Scriptures refer to Him in a number of ways. And all of them are right. Some of the names for Jesus are metaphors–just as when my teacher's husband called her "Honey."

✓ *Off the top of your head, list as many names, titles, metaphorical names that you can think of for Jesus. If you are doing this as part of a class, you may decide to do this as part of a discussion or in small groups.*

More than a Shadow of Christ. When some people look at the inspired songs, they see only shadows of Christ. Therefore, they see them as dead, powerless relics. One author said, "The Old Testament proclaimed the Father openly, and the Son more obscurely."[14] Another man stated,

The psalms do not mention the Lord Jesus except in typology. Can you imagine a church at worship and not mentioning the Lord by his name? The incarnation was not only the most amazing appearance of the person of God in history but was the fulfillment of very many OT prophecies; indeed the whole OT revelation culminated in the birth of Jesus Christ—the long promised Messiah. How can it be possible that the culmination of everything which all the OT prophets pointed forward to, that all the elect hoped for, could be ignored in songs of praise?[15]

Or as Isaac Watts, a writer of many classic hymns sung today, said, "To accommodate the book of Psalms to Christian worship...it is necessary to divest David and Asaph...and to make them always speak the...language of a Christian."[16] In other words, God's Book of Psalms needs additional man-written supplements or needs to be substantially rewritten to give substance to a "obscure" shadow of Christ. The truth could not be farther from such opinions: "It is the profound Christian persuasion that Christ

---

[14] Gregory Nazianzen, as quoted by Peter J. Naylor, "What Should We Sing," http://www.banneroftruth.org/pages/articles/article_detail.php?1414, retrieved February 5, 2013.

[15] Paul Fahy, "The Argument over 'Psalms Only'," http://understanding-ministries.co.uk/the-argument-over-psalms-only.html, retrieved February 5, 2013.

[16] Isaac Watts, *The Psalms of David Imitated in the Language of The New Testament And Applied to The Christian State and Worship*, 8.

walks within the psalms...."[17] Christ *lives* in the Psalms. In the Psalms He is fully formed and fully expressed. This chapter examines the fully formed Christ, alive in the Psalms as the Apostles saw Him there.

The High Priest: The role of the high priest under the Law of Moses was critical. Aaron was the first high priest and only his direct lineage could be a high priest. Only the high priest could enter into the Most Holy place, into the very presence of God, that he "might offer gifts and sacrifices for sins." Hebrews 5:1. But we know that Christ is now our High Priest. Hebrews 5. But the proof that Christ is the High Priest comes from Psalm 110:4: "The Lord has sworn and will not relent, 'You *are* a priest forever according to the order of Melchizedek.'" It is interesting to look at the tense of the verb–it is in the *present* tense. Therefore, Aaron, the first high priest, is a shadow of Christ. Hebrews 5-9.

The King: Jesus Himself says that He is the King of the Jews: a point so important that it is recorded in all four Gospels. Matthew 27:11, Mark 15:2, Luke 23:3 and John 18:37. Paul describes Christ as "King of kings and Lord of lords."[18] 1 Timothy 6:15. For example, when Jesus made His "triumphal entry" into Jerusalem, the crowds quoted prophetically from Psalm 118: 25-26: "Save now, I pray, O Lord....Blessed *is* he who comes in the name of the Lord!" In Luke 19:38, this Psalm is quoted as "Blessed is the King who comes in the name of the Lord." Psalm 24 is also an account of this same event. God states, "Lift up your heads, O gates, and lift them up, O ancient doors, that the King of glory may come in! Who is this King of glory? The Lord of hosts, He is the King of glory." Psalm 24:9-10.[19] Throughout the Psalms, the King of Israel–the King of the Jews–is glorified. You cannot read Psalm 72 and imagine it applying to an earthly king: "May his name endure forever; May his name increase as long as the sun shines. And let

---

[17] Patrick Henry Reardon, *Christ in the Psalms*, xvi.

[18] "Lord of lords" is a phrase quoted from Psalm 136:3.

[19] Speaking of this event, Zechariah said, "Rejoice greatly, O daughter of Zion! Shout, O daughter of Jerusalem! Behold, your King is coming to you; He *is* just and having salvation, Lowly and riding on a donkey, A colt, the foal of a donkey." Zechariah 9:9. When Christ entered with praise as prophesied, the city asked, "Who is this?" echoing the question in Psalm 24, "Who is this King of glory?" Matthew 21:10.

men bless themselves by him; Let all the nations call him blessed."[20] Psalm 72:17. When you see a reference to the king in the Psalms, it is referring to *the* King.[21]

The Son: God refers to Jesus as his Son in Psalm 2:7 when He says, "You *are* My Son, today I have begotten You." The writer of Hebrews directly identifies the "Son" as Jesus Christ. Hebrews 5:5. In fact, all of Psalm 2 is about Christ. As followers of Christ, *we* are mentioned in verse 12: "How blessed are all who take refuge in [the Son]!" But rather than being a fleeting shadow of the past, we have a declaration of the present: notice the words "today" and "you are." Jesus also referred to Himself as the "Son of Man." Matthew 9:6 and Mark 14:21. The Holy Spirit calls Jesus the "Son of Man" in Psalm 8 and Psalm 144. "What is man that You are mindful of him, and the son of man that You visit him? For You have made him a little lower than the angels, and You have crowned him with glory and honor." Psalm 8:4-5. In fact, this song is proof that Jesus is the Christ, the Son and the King. Hebrews 2:5-9. The verbs in Psalm 8 are in *present tense*. When we sing this Praise today, we are singing about Christ as He is.

The Rock: One of the most amazing and wonderful shadows God gave us is His image of Jesus as a "rock" or a "stone." Psalm 114 is an amazing story of God's redemption of His people. Both our baptism and our overcoming sin and death are described here. See 1 Corinthians 10:1-4. Notice the wonderful description of our Lord and Christ at the end of Psalm 114: "Tremble, O earth, before the Lord, Before the God of Jacob, Who turned the rock into a pool of water, The flint into a fountain of water." Jesus is that Rock. "For they drank of that spiritual Rock that followed them, and that Rock was Christ." 1 Corinthians 10:4. Jesus told the Samaritan woman at the well, "Whoever drinks of this water will thirst again, but whoever drinks of the water that I shall give him will never thirst. But the water that I shall give him will become in him a fountain of water springing up into everlasting life." John 4:13-14. Jesus is the Rock and the source of that "living water." When we sing Psalm 114, we sing of salvation through Christ and the life we have only through Him.

---

[20] Psalm 72:15 specifically mentions gold from Sheba being given to the King, which is repeated in Isaiah 60:6 and fulfilled in Matthew 2:11.

[21] The angel Gabriel said of Christ, "...the Lord God will give Him the throne of His father David; and He will reign over the house of Jacob forever; and His kingdom will have no end." Luke 1:33-33.

Jesus is also the "cornerstone." Jesus is wonderfully described and exalted: "The stone *which* the builders rejected has become the chief cornerstone." Psalm 118: 22-23. Jesus, Peter and Paul all say that the cornerstone is Jesus Christ. Matthew 21:41-44, Acts 4:10-12 and Ephesians 2:20. And again, notice the tenses in the song: "the builders *rejected*" and "*has become*": the Holy Spirit wrote this song to be sung today, after these events occurred.

The Shepherd: Jesus said twice, "I am the good shepherd." John 10:11-16. Jesus did not just say he was a shepherd, but "I *am* the good shepherd." For many people, this saying instantly calls to mind one of the most famous songs, "The LORD is my shepherd." So who is it that leads us beside still waters? It's Jesus. Jesus said in effect, "That's Me in that song." Not only there, but Psalm 80 begins: "Give ear, O Shepherd of Israel, You who lead Joseph like a flock...Stir up Your strength, And come and save us!" Who is the Savior? He is none other than the Good Shepherd. With this wonderful description of Christ as the Good Shepherd, the last verse of Psalm 119 ends with even greater power. It ends with our plea for salvation: "I have gone astray like a lost sheep; Seek Your servant, For I do not forget Your commandments."[22]

We haven't seen anything yet! It is impossible to point out Christ in all the corners, nooks and crannies of the Psalms where He is mentioned. If we act like kindergarteners and know Him only as "Jesus," we shut down our understanding of who He is, all that He does, and all He will do. He is the Door through which the righteous enter. Psalm 118:19-21 and John 10:9. He is the Light. Psalm 118:27 and John 1:4-9. He is the Root that God has planted and the Branch that He has strengthened. Psalm 80:15, Isaiah 11:1-11 and Zechariah 3:8. He is the Right Hand of God. Psalm 98:1 and Psalm 118:15-19. Jesus is also known as "David." Psalm 132:1 and Ezekiel 37:24-25. As one looks closer at God's inspired songs, one sees Jesus *living* in almost every song in the book. He's not just a fleeting shadow in the Psalms: He walks through them. He lives in them.

✓ *Here is a challenge as you read or sing the Psalms in your daily study. Make a list of all the names, titles, and functions that the Spirit of Christ uses to refer to "Jesus."*

---

[22] See the Parable of the Lost Sheep to understand the line of this song more deeply. Luke 15:4-7.

✓ Sing the excerpt from Psalm 89 again that appears below. Do you notice any references to Jesus in this song that you didn't notice before? What are they?

_____

_____

Psalm 89:19-26

In vision to thy Holy One Thou saidst, I help have laid
Upon a mighty one, and from the people choice have made.
Ev'n David, I have found him out a servant unto me;
And with my holy oil my King anointed him to be.

With whom my hand shall established be; my arm shall make him strong.
On him the foe shall not exact, nor son of mischief wrong.
I will beat down before his face all his malicious foes;
I will them greatly plague who do with hatred him oppose.

My mercy and my faithfulness with him yet still shall be;
And in my name his horn and pow'r man shall exalted see.
His hand and pow'r shall reach afar, I'll set it in the sea;
And his right hand established shall upon the rivers be.

Thou art my Father and my God, He unto me shall cry;
Thou also art the Rock on which for safety I rely.
I'll make him my first born, supreme o'er kings of ev'ry land,
My love I'll ever keep for him, my cov'nant fast shall stand.

This song can be sung to the tune of "Alas! and Did My Savior Bleed?," "Be Not Dismayed Whate'er Betide (God Will Take Care of You)," "God Heal Our Land," "I Am Bound for the Promised Land (On Jordan's Stormy Banks I Stand)," "I Know My Redeemer Lives," "I Know Whom I Have Believed," "Lead Me to Calvary," "Oh, How I Love Jesus," "There Is a Fountain Filled with Blood," "There Is a Place of Quiet Rest (Near to the Heart of God)," "To Christ Be Loyal," and "We'll Work Til Jesus Comes."

7 : SEEING YOUR OWN SHADOW

Prosopagnosia is a mental disorder in which the person afflicted is unable to recognize faces, including their own. A woman suffering with this disease would not be able to recognize her own face in a mirror. After a severe accident or after recovering sight following a long period of blindness, even a sighted person may not recognize her own face in a mirror or in a photograph.

Many times we suffer from a type of spiritual prosopagnosia: we fail to recognize our own faces when we see them in the scriptures. The Book of Psalms contains many portraits of ourselves that most of us don't recognize as *us*. Because we are so used to seeing ourselves from a certain perspective or because we don't see ourselves at all, it may seem strange at first when we see ourselves as the Holy Spirit sees us. One woman had only a small mirror to see herself when she dressed; however, when she bought a full length mirror and saw her full physique, she was upset with her husband for not telling her she was fat! Quite the opposite is true for us: once we have the opportunity to see ourselves from God's perspective. Most people will be surprised–in a good way–by the perspective. When one woman's sight was restored after being blind for eleven years, looking in a mirror was a difficult experience for her: "It took me a long time to build up the courage to do that....When I finally did look at myself in the mirror it felt weird–I kept going back to see myself again and again."[23] At first, seeing ourselves in the Psalms may feel strange, but eventually we are able to see ourselves more

---

[23] "Coming to Their Senses," *The Guardian*, April 28, 2008. Section G2, page 16.

completely. So, let' s get ready to feel a little "weird." And hopefully we will keep coming back to look at ourselves "again and again."

Christians are the Nation of Israel, the Nation of Promise. Christians are called "a holy nation," but we often don't recognize what nation that is. 1 Peter 2:9. When God told Abraham that He would make him a great nation in Genesis 12:2, God did not mean that it would be merely a physical nation. God also made a *spiritual* nation out of Abraham. Paul explained this in Romans 9:6-9:

> For they are not all Israel who are of Israel, nor are they all children because they are the seed of Abraham; but, "In Isaac your seed shall be called." That is, those who are the children of the flesh, these are not the children of God; but the children of the promise are counted as the seed.

This is just as Hosea prophesied when he said that those who were "not God's people" (the gentiles or non-Jews) would be numbered with the Children of Israel and would become "sons of the living God." Hosea 1:10. Paul explained that gentiles were "grafted" into the Nation of Israel: the unbelieving Jews were cut off from the Nation and believing gentiles were made a part of the Nation. For those of us who are not from the *physical* nation of Israel, we become part of *spiritual* Israel so that God's word will be fulfilled: "All Israel will be saved." Romans 11:11-27. God said,

> Behold, the days are coming, says the Lord, when I will make *a new covenant with the house of Israel and with the house of Judah*....But this *is* the covenant that I will make *with the house of Israel* after those days, says the Lord: I will put My law in their minds, and write it on their hearts; and I will be their God, and they shall be My people....

(emphasis supplied.) Jeremiah 31:31-34. With whom would the covenant be made? With the house of Israel and the house of Judah. But because the non-Jews have been grafted into Israel, the covenant is with us, spiritual Israel, too.

The previous chapter pointed out that Jesus was our Shepherd. But, Jesus is the Shepherd of Israel. In Matthew 2:6, Micah is quoted as saying "...For out of [Bethlehem] shall come a Ruler Who will shepherd My people Israel." If this prophecy applies only to the physical Nation of Israel, it portrays Jesus with limited influence. But today Jesus rules and shepherds the *spiritual* nation of Israel: Jesus rules and shepherds us as the church.[24]

But, Paul explained it very succinctly: "Now we, brethren, as Isaac was, are children of promise." Galatians 4:28. And this fact makes Psalm 105:5-6 even more powerful for us today:

> Remember His marvelous works which He has done,
> His wonders, and the judgments of His mouth,
> O seed of Abraham His servant,
> You children of Jacob, His chosen ones!

✓ *After reading the passage above, were you able to see yourself?*

_____

_____

The Christians are the Tabernacle and Temple of God both individually and collectively. The place where God "dwelled" in the Old Testament was first the Tabernacle and then the Temple. But now God dwells in us as Christians; we have become His Temple. Paul explained this very clearly: "For you are the temple of the living God." 2 Corinthians 6:16. And again, "Do you not know that you are the temple of God and *that* the Spirit of God dwells in you? If anyone defiles the temple of God, God will destroy him. For the temple of God is holy, which *temple* you are." 1 Corinthians 3:16-17. Individually, if we have been baptized and are raised to be alive spiritually, we have God dwelling in us: "But if the Spirit of Him who raised Jesus from the dead dwells in you, He who raised Christ from the dead will also give life to your mortal bodies through His Spirit who dwells in you." Romans 8:11. Therefore, we are then a spiritual tabernacle or temple for God: we are a "tabernacle not made with hands, that is, not of this creation." Hebrews 9:11.[25]

Because the Holy Spirit gives us spiritual life, we have become "living stones." Peter says that we are being built into a spiritual house with Christ being the Cornerstone. 1 Peter 2:4-8. Paul says that we are being built into "a holy temple in the Lord...[and] built together for a dwelling

_____

[24] Jesus said, "My kingdom is not of this world." John 18:36.

[25] Christians are spiritual creatures born of the Spirit. John 3:5-6.

place of God in the Spirit." Ephesians 2:19-22. God said that when He makes the New Covenant, He would dwell in our "midst forevermore:"

> Moreover I will make a covenant of peace with them, and it shall be an everlasting covenant with them; I will establish them and multiply them, and I will set My sanctuary in their midst forevermore. My tabernacle also shall be with them; indeed I will be their God, and they shall be My people. The nations also will know that I, the Lord, sanctify Israel, when My sanctuary is in their midst forevermore.

Ezekiel 37:26-28. What God didn't reveal at that time was that His Tabernacle would be the very hearts of His people. This realization gives more power as we see ourselves portrayed in Revelation 21:3: "Behold, the tabernacle of God *is* with men, and He will dwell with them, and they shall be His people. God Himself will be with them *and be* their God."

So when we sing, "In my distress I called upon the Lord, And cried out to my God; *He heard my voice from His temple*, And my cry came before Him, *even* to His ears," we know that God is very close to us–actually inside us–hearing our cries and pleas. Psalm 18:6. When we sing Psalm 46, we realize that we are singing of the help and protection that God gives to us.

Then, how does God view His dwelling places and His temples? "How lovely are Your dwelling places, O LORD of hosts!" Psalm 84:1.

√ *Read these lines from Psalm 46. Do you see yourself? If so, what does this mean for you?*

> There is a river whose streams shall make glad the city of God,
> The holy place of the tabernacle of the Most High.
>
> God *is* in the midst of her, she shall not be moved;
> God shall help her, just at the break of dawn.[26]

---

[26] See also Ezekiel's description of the spiritual temple with the river flowing from it (Ezekiel 40-47) and the city in Revelation with the river flowing from the throne (Revelation 21:1-22:5). There is no river in or near earthly Jerusalem.

The Church is Jerusalem and Mount Zion. God set up the city of Jerusalem as the capital city for the Nation of Israel. It was there, on Mount Zion, in Jerusalem, that He chose to build his earthly Temple. But we must realize that Jerusalem was chosen because it was a symbol of what was to come, the assembly of the saved of God. We see that we are the spiritual Jerusalem because we are the church:

> But you have come to Mount Zion and to the city of the living God, the heavenly Jerusalem, to an innumerable company of angels, to the general assembly and church of the firstborn who are registered in heaven....

Hebrews 12:22-23. The word "firstborn" refers to us.[27] We are those who were born in Zion. Psalm 87:5-6. We are Mount Zion and the heavenly Jerusalem. "Walk about Zion, and go around her...that you may tell it to the next generation." Psalm 48:12-13. Paul even emphasizes this more when he compares the old covenant with the new covenant: "...for this Hagar is Mount Sinai in Arabia, and corresponds to Jerusalem which now is, and is in bondage with her children—*but the Jerusalem above is free, which is the mother of us all.*" Galatians 4:25-26 Paul's explanation gives Psalm 87 added relevancy: "And of Zion it will be said, "This *one* and that *one* were born in her...." Then in Revelation, God *shows* us that the New Jerusalem is the church *and* the tabernacle: "Then I, John, saw the holy city, New Jerusalem, coming down out of heaven from God, prepared as a bride adorned for her husband. And I heard a loud voice from heaven saying, 'Behold, the tabernacle of God *is* with men, and He will dwell with them, and they shall be His people. God Himself will be with them *and be* their God.'" Revelation 21:2-3.[28]

We are Kings and Royalty as brothers and sisters of the King. There is no doubt that Jesus Christ is the King of Kings. But, as Christians and adopted sons, we have become royalty, too. Peter calls us "a royal priesthood." 1 Peter 2:9. And Paul gives us an inkling of our royal status when he said, "If we endure, We shall also *reign* with Him." 2 Timothy 2:12. Christ also tells us this in Revelation 3:21: "To him who overcomes I will grant to sit with Me on My throne, as I also overcame and sat down with My Father on His throne." But John, makes it clear that Christ has already made us kings: "To Him who loved us and washed us from our

---

[27] "Firstborn" in this instance is neuter in gender and plural and cannot refer to Christ.

[28] God dwells with us now: 1 Corinthians 3:16, Romans 8:9 and 11, 2 Timothy 1:14, James 4:5; Jesus, Ephesians 3:17 Galatians 2:20, 2 John 9, 1 John 4:15-16.

sins in His own blood, and has made us kings and priests to His God and Father, to Him *be* glory and dominion forever and ever." Revelation 1:5-6.

✓ *Read these sentences from Psalm 132. Do you see yourself? If so, what does this mean for you?*

> For Your servant David's sake,[29]
> Do not turn away the face of Your Anointed.
> The Lord has sworn *in* truth to David;
> He will not turn from it:
> "I will set upon your throne the fruit of your body.
> If your sons will keep My covenant
> And My testimony which I shall teach them,
> Their sons also shall sit upon your throne forevermore...."

Christians are Priests and the Tribe of Levi. The scriptures referenced in the last chapter pointed to Christ as our High Priest. But *we* are also priests. John said that Christ "has loved us and washed us from our sins in His own blood, and has made us kings and priests to His God and Father." Revelation 1:5-6. The Law of Moses was "symbolic for the present time" regarding the priesthood. Hebrews 9:9. Peter said that we "are...a holy priesthood, to offer up spiritual sacrifices acceptable to God through Jesus Christ" and "a royal priesthood." 1 Peter 2:4-5, 9.

As priests, we offer sacrifices. Many Christians mistakenly think that sacrifices ceased when the Old Covenant was fulfilled. Although there is now no more sacrifice for sin under Christ (Hebrews 10:26), Christians do–or should–make sacrifices. Peter said that as priests, we "offer up spiritual sacrifices acceptable to God through Jesus Christ." 1 Peter 2:5. The following are examples of sacrifices under the New Covenant:

- our bodies as living sacrifices–Romans 12:1.
- praise to God–Hebrews 13:15.
- giving thanks to God–Hebrews 13:15.
- aid we give other Christians–Philippians 4:14-18.

---

[29] The scriptures sometimes prophetically refer toJesus as "David." Ezekiel 37:24-25.

- service to other Christians–Philippians 2:17.
- doing good and sharing–Hebrews 13:16.

As priests, we partake of the sacrifice. Christ has taken the place of the animal sacrifices so that now there is no need for sacrifices for sin. But we as priests, partake of what was sacrificed when we take the Lord's Supper: Paul points out that the Lord's Supper is the same as the priest's partaking of what was sacrificed: "The cup of blessing which we bless, is it not the communion of the blood of Christ? The bread which we break, is it not the communion of the body of Christ? For we, *though* many, are one bread *and* one body; for we all partake of that one bread. Observe Israel after the flesh: Are not those who eat of the sacrifices partakers of the altar?" 1 Corinthians 10:16-18. Under the Law of Moses, only the priests ate of the sacrifices. The very act of eating the Lord's Supper, Communion, is a priestly act.

✓ *Read these two verses: Psalm 132:9 and 16.[36] Do you see yourself? If so, what does this mean for you?*

> Let Your priests be clothed with righteousness,
> And let Your saints shout for joy....
>
> I will also clothe her priests with salvation,
> And her saints shall shout aloud for joy.

We are Christ's Bride. Jesus is repeatedly referred to as a bridegroom.[30] But who is He marrying? Us. Paul said that we are betrothed (or engaged) to Christ: "For I am jealous for you with godly jealousy. For I have betrothed you to one husband, that I may present *you as* a chaste virgin to Christ." 2 Corinthians 11:2. Paul said that we had become dead to the law so that we could be married to Christ. Romans 7:4. In fact, when Paul describes the whole relationship between a husband and wife, he said what he was really talking about was Christ and the church, with His church being His bride. Ephesians 5:32.

Some people have said that a woman is the most beautiful when she is a bride walking down the aisle about to be wed to her husband. And this is the picture that God gives us in the book of Revelation: "Then I, John,

---

[30] Matthew 9:15, Mark 2:19, Luke 5:34, and John 3:29.

saw the holy city, New Jerusalem, coming down out of heaven from God, prepared as a bride adorned for her husband....Then one of the seven angels...talked with me, saying, 'Come, I will show you the bride, the Lamb's wife.' And he carried me away in the Spirit to a great and high mountain, and showed me the great city, the holy Jerusalem, descending out of heaven from God, having the glory of God." Rev. 21:2, 9-11.[31]

✓ *Read these lines from Psalm 45. Do you see yourself? If so, what does this mean for you? You look pretty good, don't you?*

> Listen, O daughter,
> Consider and incline your ear;
> Forget your own people also, and your father's house;
>
> So the King will greatly desire your beauty;
> Because He *is* your Lord, worship Him...
>
> The royal daughter *is* all glorious within *the palace;*
> Her clothing *is* woven with gold.
>
> She shall be brought to the King in robes of many colors....

_____

_____

✓ *Read these sentences from Psalm 135:19-21. If you are with a group, try reading this passage aloud together. Or, you may choose to use it as a responsive reading with the leader saying the bold, and the rest of the group reading the regular type.*

> **Bless the Lord,** O house of Israel!
> **Bless the Lord,** O house of Aaron!
> **Bless the Lord,** O house of Levi!
> **You who fear the Lord,** bless the Lord!
> **Blessed be the Lord** out of Zion,
> **Who dwells in Jerusalem!** Praise the Lord!

✓ *Do you see yourself? In how many ways are you described?*

_____

_____

---

[31] This is not promissory: we have that Glory now by the transforming power of the Spirit of the Lord. 2 Corinthians 3:18.

8:CHRIST'S SUFFERINGS

Chomolungma has taken the lives of many men and women who have tried to conquer her. Along the way to her summit, dead bodies lie untouched and unburied. The route is so dangerous and inaccessible that no one can honor the fallen. In anguish and pain, men and women trudge past the bodies as they try to cheat death themselves. Twenty-four hours on May 10-11, 1996 was the most deadly on Chomolungma: she took eight lives. Chomolungma is the mountain's name in the language of Tibet. We know her as Mount Everest.

As men and women were climbing on May 10, 1996, the base camp below was filled with observers. A film crew, making a movie of an ascent of Everest, photographed the climbers from a distance through telephoto lenses. Through radios, the observers could hear the voices of the climbers as they struggled and died. But no one seeing and hearing from the base camp could know what the climbers felt, saw and heard– and we might never have known except someone lived through it. An author, commissioned to document the summiting of Everest, was among the climbers that day. Narrowly escaping death himself, he documented the events *he* experienced: the pain of searing cold *he* felt, the death and suffering *he* saw, and the dying climbers' whimpers and the screaming winds *he* heard. [32]

The Mind of Christ. One dictionary defines "mind" as "the element...in an individual that feels, perceives, thinks, wills, and especially reasons." Who knows Christ's thoughts and feelings as He was being betrayed?

---

[32] Jon Krakauer documented this disaster in his book, *Into Thin Air*.

Who knows His feelings as His closest friends abandoned Him? Who knows His feelings as He was beaten and then nailed to a cross? Who knows His thoughts as even God forsook Him? As observers, we can only "see" what happened and "hear" what He said. As mere observers, we cannot know. But we have an observer who felt, saw and heard Christ's sufferings. The Holy Spirit has opened up to us the deep feelings and emotions of Christ in the Book of Psalms.

Only God Himself knows what Christ experienced.

> But God has revealed [the things He has prepared for us] to us through His Spirit. For the Spirit searches all things, yes, the deep things of God. For what man knows the things of a man except the spirit of the man which is in him? Even so no one knows the things of God except the Spirit of God....

1 Corinthians 2:10-16. Paul tells us that Christ should dwell in our hearts so that we can understand "the width and length and depth and height" of Christ's love, a love that passes "knowledge" and so that we may "be filled with all the fullness of God." Ephesians 3:16-19. Understanding the depths of both His physical *and* mental sufferings helps us begin to comprehend the depth of His love: the greatness of His suffering demonstrates the greatness of His love. Because the New Testament is nearly silent on Christ's thoughts and feelings, how can we really begin to understand the magnitude of Christ's love? Paul says that as spiritual creatures, we are to have the mind of Christ. 1 Corinthians 2:16. And Peter tells us to arm ourselves with the same mind as the suffering Christ:

> Therefore, since Christ suffered for us in the flesh, *arm yourselves also with the same mind*, for he who has suffered in the flesh has ceased from sin, that he no longer should live the rest of *his* time in the flesh for the lusts of men, but for the will of God.

1 Peter 4:1-2. Matthew, Mark, Luke and John do not describe Christ's mind, feelings or thoughts: there we see mostly His actions.

The Spirit fully understands Christ's Sufferings. Jesus was "a man of sorrows and acquainted with grief." Isaiah 53:3. How can we understand the great love He had so that we can even begin to understand those sorrows and griefs? We have a problem similar to the observers of the Everest climbers from base camp: we can see and hear, but we can't truly understand unless the mind of one of those sufferers is revealed to us. Only the Spirit intimately knows the mind of God; therefore, He fully comprehends Christ's love, Christ's suffering and Christ's consolations. Only He can relate to us the deep, emotional thoughts of Christ.

In Psalm 41:9, the Holy Spirit wrote: "Even my own familiar friend in whom I trusted, Who ate my bread, Has lifted up *his* heel against me." At the Last Supper, Christ quoted from this Psalm: "I do not speak concerning all of you. I know whom I have chosen; but that the Scripture may be fulfilled, 'He who eats bread with Me has lifted up his heel against Me.'" John 13:18. Because Christ is Deity and knew that Judas was ready to betray Him, He left off the phrase "in whom I trusted." Many scholars have seen this as a proof of Christ's divinity.

√ *Sing Psalm 88 that appears on page 55. If you are studying in a class or a group, you may wish to sing a few verses if time is an issue. (The suggested verses are in bold.)*

√ *In your words, what is the extent of Christ's grief in Psalm 88?*

_____

_____

Christ's quotes from the Cross. Our first hints that Christ's innermost thoughts are contained in the Psalms come from Christ himself. How do we know that the emotional outpourings in the Psalms belong to our Savior? We know this because Christ quoted directly from the Psalms. He said, "My God, my God, why have you forsaken me?" Psalm 22. And He said, "Into your hands I commit my spirit." Psalm 31. Christ expresses His painful, agonizing thoughts. "Let this mind be in you which was also in Christ Jesus...He humbled Himself and became obedient to *the point of* death, even the death of the cross." Philippians 2:5-8. Let's look into that great mind.

Excerpts from the Gospels stating the factual event that happened follow. Next to each event are the expression of emotions that Christ experienced.

Gospel Account	Christ's Thoughts
The leaders plot Jesus's death. **Mark 14:1** And the chief priests and the scribes sought how they might take Him by trickery and put *Him* to death.	**Psalm 41:5-8** My enemies speak evil of me: "When will he die, and his name perish?" And if he comes to see *me,* he speaks lies; His heart gathers iniquity to itself; *When* he goes out, he tells *it.* All who hate me whisper together against me; Against me they devise my hurt. "An evil disease," *they say,* "clings to him. And *now* that he lies down, he will rise up no more."
Jesus is put on trial. **Mark 14:46, 50, 53-64** Then they laid their hands on Him and took Him....Then they all forsook Him and fled. And they led Jesus away to the high priest; and with him were assembled all the chief priests, the elders, and the scribes....Now the chief priests and all the council sought testimony against Jesus to put Him to death, but found none. For many bore false witness against Him, but their testimonies did not agree.... And the high priest stood up in the midst and asked Jesus, saying, "Do You answer nothing? What *is it* these men testify against You?" But He kept silent and answered nothing. **The term "iniquity" here means "guilt or punishment of iniquity" or "punishment for iniquity" in Hebrew. (Strong's H5771 - 'avon) Christ is not saying He has committed sin, but that He is suffering punishment because of sin. Or, an even more loving explanation, this song demonstrates an unfathomable aspect of Christ's love. We know that Christ "bore our sins" and became "sin on our behalf." 1 Peter 2:24 and 2 Corinthians 5:21. Christ so loved us that He took on our sins and our punishment, that He called our sins His own.*	**Psalm 31:9-13** Have mercy on me, O Lord, for I am in trouble; My eye wastes away with grief, *Yes,* my soul and my body! For my life is spent with grief, And my years with sighing; My strength fails because of my iniquity,* And my bones waste away. I am a reproach among all my enemies, But especially among my neighbors, And *am* repulsive to my acquaintances; Those who see me outside flee from me. I am forgotten like a dead man, out of mind; I am like a broken vessel. For I hear the slander of many; Fear *is* on every side; While they take counsel together against me, They scheme to take away my life. **Psalm 64:1-6** Hear my voice, O God, in my meditation; Preserve my life from fear of the enemy. Hide me from the secret plots of the wicked, From the rebellion of the workers of iniquity, Who sharpen their tongue like a sword, And bend *their bows to shoot* their arrows—bitter words, That they may shoot in secret at the blameless; Suddenly they shoot at him and do not fear. They encourage themselves *in* an evil matter; They talk of laying snares secretly; They say, "Who will see them?" They devise iniquities: "We have perfected a shrewd scheme." Both the inward thought and the heart of man are deep. **Psalm 38:12-14** Those also who seek my life lay snares *for me;* Those who seek my hurt speak of destruction, And plan deception all the day long. But I, like a deaf *man,* do not hear; And *I am* like a mute *who* does not open his mouth. Thus I am like a man who does not hear, And in whose mouth *is* no response.

Gospel Account	Christ's Thoughts
Jesus is tortured. **Luke 22:63-65** Now the men who held Jesus mocked Him and beat Him. And having blindfolded Him, they struck Him on the face and asked Him, saying, "Prophesy! Who is the one who struck You?" And many other things they blasphemously spoke against Him. **Matthew 27:27-30** Then the soldiers of the governor took Jesus into the Praetorium and gathered the whole garrison around Him. And they stripped Him and put a scarlet robe on Him. When they had twisted a crown of thorns, they put *it* on His head, and a reed in His right hand. And they bowed the knee before Him and mocked Him, saying, "Hail, King of the Jews!" Then they spat on Him, and took the reed and struck Him on the head.	**Psalm 38:1-11, 15-20** O Lord, do not rebuke me in Your wrath, Nor chasten me in Your hot displeasure! For Your arrows pierce me deeply, And Your hand presses me down. *There is* no soundness in my flesh Because of Your anger, Nor *any* health in my bones Because of my sin.* For my iniquities* have gone over my head; Like a heavy burden they are too heavy for me. My wounds are foul *and* festering Because of my foolishness. I am troubled, I am bowed down greatly; I go mourning all the day long. For my loins are full of inflammation, And *there is* no soundness in my flesh. I am feeble and severely broken; I groan because of the turmoil of my heart. Lord, all my desire *is* before You; And my sighing is not hidden from You. My heart pants, my strength fails me; As for the light of my eyes, it also has gone from me. My loved ones and my friends stand aloof from my plague, And my relatives stand afar off... For in You, O Lord, I hope; You will hear, O Lord my God. For I said, *"Hear me,* lest they rejoice over me, Lest, when my foot slips, they exalt *themselves* against me." For I *am* ready to fall, And my sorrow *is* continually before me. For I will declare my iniquity; I will be in anguish over my sin.* But my enemies *are* vigorous, *and* they are strong; And those who hate me wrongfully have multiplied. Those also who render evil for good, They are my adversaries, because I follow *what is* good. **Psalm 57:4 and 6** My soul *is* among lions; I lie *among* the sons of men Who are set on fire, Whose teeth *are* spears and arrows, And their tongue a sharp sword... They have prepared a net for my steps; My soul is bowed down; They have dug a pit before me;....
*The terms "sin" and "iniquity" here mean "guilt or punishment of iniquity" or "punishment for iniquity" in Hebrew. (Strong's H5771 - 'avon) As in Psalm 31, Christ is not saying He has committed sin, but that He is being punished because of sin.	

Gospel Account	Christ's Thoughts
Jesus is crucified. **John 19:17-18, 23-24, 28** And He, bearing His cross, went out to a place called *the Place* of a Skull, which is called in Hebrew, Golgotha, where they crucified Him, and two others with Him, one on either side, and Jesus in the center. Then the soldiers, when they had crucified Jesus, took His garments and made four parts, to each soldier a part, and also the tunic. Now the tunic was without seam, woven from the top in one piece. They said therefore among themselves, "Let us not tear it, but cast lots for it, whose it shall be...." After this, Jesus, knowing that all things were now accomplished, that the Scripture might be fulfilled, said, "I thirst!"	**Psalm 22:11-19** Be not far from Me, For trouble *is* near; For *there is* none to help. Many bulls have surrounded Me; Strong *bulls* of Bashan have encircled Me. They gape at Me *with* their mouths, *Like* a raging and roaring lion. I am poured out like water, And all My bones are out of joint; My heart is like wax; It has melted within Me. My strength is dried up like a potsherd, And My tongue clings to My jaws; You have brought Me to the dust of death. For dogs have surrounded Me; The congregation of the wicked has enclosed Me. They pierced My hands and My feet; I can count all My bones. They look *and* stare at Me. They divide My garments among them, And for My clothing they cast lots. But You, O Lord, do not be far from Me; O My Strength, hasten to help Me!
Jesus is mocked. **Mark 15:29-32** And those who passed by blasphemed Him, wagging their heads and saying, "Aha! *You* who destroy the temple and build *it* in three days, save Yourself, and come down from the cross!" Likewise the chief priests also, mocking among themselves with the scribes, said, "He saved others; Himself He cannot save. Let the Christ, the King of Israel, descend now from the cross, that we may see and believe." Even those who were crucified with Him reviled Him.	**Psalm 22:6-8** But I *am* a worm, and no man; A reproach of men, and despised by the people. All those who see Me ridicule Me; They shoot out the lip, they shake the head, *saying,* "He trusted in the Lord, let Him rescue Him; Let Him deliver Him, since He delights in Him!"

Gospel Account	Christ's Thoughts
The earth quakes. **Matthew 27:51-52** Then, behold, the veil of the temple was torn in two from top to bottom; and the earth quaked, and the rocks were split, and the graves were opened; and many bodies of the saints who had fallen asleep were raised... **Luke 23:44-45** Now it was about the sixth hour, and there was darkness over all the earth until the ninth hour. Then the sun was darkened, and the veil of the temple was torn in two.	**Psalm 18:4-15** The pangs of death surrounded me, And the floods of ungodliness made me afraid. The sorrows of Sheol surrounded me; The snares of death confronted me. In my distress I called upon the Lord, And cried out to my God; He heard my voice from His temple, And my cry came before Him, *even* to His ears. Then the earth shook and trembled; The foundations of the hills also quaked and were shaken, Because He was angry. Smoke went up from His nostrils, And devouring fire from His mouth; Coals were kindled by it. He bowed the heavens also, and came down With darkness under His feet. And He rode upon a cherub, and flew; He flew upon the wings of the wind. He made darkness His secret place; His canopy around Him *was* dark waters *And* thick clouds of the skies. From the brightness before Him, His thick clouds passed with hailstones and coals of fire. The Lord thundered from heaven, And the Most High uttered His voice, Hailstones and coals of fire. He sent out His arrows and scattered the foe, Lightnings in abundance, and He vanquished them. Then the channels of the sea were seen, The foundations of the world were uncovered At Your rebuke, O Lord, At the blast of the breath of Your nostrils.

✓ *What facts or details are included in the first person account of Jesus's suffering that are not included in the third person, objective version of these events?*

_____

_____

✓ *Which account gives you an emotional understanding of Christ's suffering?*

_____

_____

Flashback. In Chapter 2 we discussed that one purpose of song was to imbed the words and thoughts of the song into the mind of the singer. In this chapter we focused on the emotional content of these Psalms; but we should not lose sight that these are not mere emotional expressions. These songs are emotional expressions that God intended for people to sing.

✓ *Why did the Holy Spirit put Christ's deepest emotional expressions in songs? When would these songs have had their greatest impact and meaning–before or after the crucifixion?*

_____

_____

✓ *Below is a version of Psalm 88. Sing the song again. If you are with a group, discuss the depth of the emotions expressed here. How do the expressions of Christ's emotions by the Holy Spirit compare with our efforts to express them?*

_____

_____

PSALM 88

God of my health to thee my prayer I make
In the bright morn and in the evening gloom:
Hear me and save! Afflictions o'er me break,
And my soul sinks with sorrow to the tomb.

As if the grave had closed above my head,
As if of strength and hope and breath bereft,
Outcast of men they count me with the dead,
Rent from thy hand and lone and helpless left.

Plunged in a dark abyss of wretchedness,
Dark as the night immeasurably deep,
Hard on my soul thy angry terrors press,
And o'er me all thy surging billows sweep.

My friends deny me as a man unknown,
Or from my hated sight abhorrent flee;
In gloomy dungeon pent, I pine alone,
Nor beam of light, nor hope of freedom see.

Mine eye with grief is wasted: every day
To thee I pour my cries, my hands I raise
Wilt thou thy wonders to the dead display?
Shall the cold dead arise and speak thy praise?

Shall all thy goodness in the grave be told?
Thy truth, where death and desolation dwell?
Thy wonders shall obscurity unfold?
Or mute oblivion all thy justice tell?

But, Lord, to thee my earnest prayer I make,
My voice salutes thee with the dawning day:
My God, my God, ah, why my soul forsake?
Why close thine ear, and turn thy face away?

E'en from my youth affliction wrings my frame,
Pain drowns my breath, and doubt distracts my soul;
Whilst, armed for death I see thy anger's flame,
And through the ravening storm thy thunders roll.

Fierce as a flood, thy terrors round me rise,
A circling sea of woes without a shore;
Each friend and lover at thy bidding flies,
And old associates go, and turn no more.

This song can be sung to the tune of "Abide with Me," "Break Now the Bread of Life," or "God of our Fathers" (National Hymn).

9:CONSOLATION

AND

PRAISE

Early in the morning on March 14, 2010, Enkosi Manenekazi was praying as she walked through her encampment in South Africa. Suddenly a man attacked her, robbed her, dragged her into a field while strangling her, and then raped her. Her attacker made three attempts to murder her during the brutal battery. Through all of this she remained calm. Finally she was released and started to heal by looking for purpose in her suffering. How was this woman able to keep calm in the face of death and brutality and then emerge, ultimately, a stronger person? She looked to the crucifixion of Christ and His deliverance by God for her consolation and strength.

Purposeless suffering strikes us all as sadistic and meaningless. Manenekazi looked for purpose in suffering: her role model was Christ. In a speech on Women's Day in South Africa in 2010, she offered hope to women in Africa and to all people. Looking to God she said, "He [God] allowed him [Christ] to be treated in an unthinkable way, this all for the biggest purpose of all, our salvation." She also said,

> As women, especially women of Africa, we have all experienced some form of suffering...We should not lower to the ground; we must pick up our cross everyday for it has a purpose. It can be very difficult, but we will not be overcome by suffering, because suffering without purpose is torture! How do we find the strength?: "And be not grieved and depressed, for the joy of the Lord is your strength and stronghold." (Nehemiah 8:9-11) This is how we are able to be happy, contagiously so...."

In a world filled with pain and suffering, we can conquer our sufferings by finding the same comfort that Christ received when He suffered for each one of us. In doing so, we can find purpose and meaning in our sufferings so that we can endure them, too.[33]

Suffering without comfort is only torture. We are blessed that the Spirit knows the "deep things" of Christ that humans cannot know: the Spirit of Christ, the Holy Spirit, has revealed the innermost feelings, thoughts and pain of Christ to us. God passionately unfolds His pain in the Psalms. But along with these intense sufferings, we also have the glorious consolations that Christ had and that He wants us to realize, too. This passionate, personal comforting is recorded nowhere more profoundly in the scriptures than in the Psalms.

When we "arm ourselves with the same mind" as the suffering Christ, we also have access to the same comforting that Christ had. The gospels do not reveal that Christ received any comfort prior to or during His death. "An angel from heaven appeared to Him, strengthening Him." Notice that the angel *strengthened* Him but did not comfort Him. The angel strengthened Him so that He could grieve and suffer more. Luke 22:43-44. God will console and comfort us:

...the Father of mercies and God of all comfort,... comforts us in all our tribulation, that we may be able to comfort those who are in any trouble, with the comfort with which we ourselves are comforted by God. For as the sufferings of Christ abound in us, so our consolation also abounds through Christ...we know that as you are partakers of the sufferings, so also you will partake of the consolation.

2 Corinthians 1:3-7.

So where is this "comfort"?

Yes, we had the sentence of death in ourselves, that we should not trust in ourselves but in God who raises the dead, who delivered us from so great a death, and does deliver us; in whom we trust that He will still deliver us....

2 Corinthians 1:9-10.

---

[33] Enkosi Manenekazi, "Suffering with Purpose," http://www.rape.co.za/index.php?option=com_content&view=article&id=1339:suffering-with-purpose-&catid=50:submitted-stories&Itemid=136, retrieved February 5, 2013.

But just as Christ's innermost agonizing, suffering thoughts are in the Psalms, so Christ's deepest and most profound consolation and comfort are found there. And that comfort is ours, too.

✓ *Sing Psalm 34, which is on page 63. This song specifically refers to Christ: John 19:36. If you are studying this book as part of a class or group and have time limitations, you may wish to sing in bold.*

Our comfort is best expressed in the Psalms. Many people throughout the ages have suffered. Many people throughout the ages have also been comforted by one thing, or idea or philosophy. Throughout Christ's sufferings, we see *how* He was comforted and *who* comforts and consoles. Just as Enkosi Manenekaz knew when she was enduring her abuse, the comfort that we can have in our suffering is God's love and protection for us. Our comfort is in Christ through the Holy Spirit. Philippians 2:1 and Acts 9:31. God's love and protection for us is ultimately demonstrated in the resurrection of Christ: His ultimate triumph over death and *all* enemies. As Christians, we participate in that same love and protection. Paul explained, "Yes, we had the sentence of death in ourselves, that we should not trust in ourselves but in God who raises the dead, who delivered us from so great a death, and does deliver us; in whom we trust that He will still deliver us..." 2 Corinthians 1:9-10. In quoting Psalm 69, Paul directs us to the source of our comfort: the scriptures. "For even Christ did not please Himself; but as it is written, 'The reproaches of those who reproached You fell on Me.' For whatever things were written before were written for our learning, that we through the patience and *comfort of the Scriptures* might have hope." Romans 15:3-4. In the same way as the Holy Spirit reveals Christ's intimate, emotional expressions of suffering in the Psalms, the Spirit also reveals Christ's intimate, emotional expressions of faith, assurance, and comfort there.

In Psalm 16, Christ expresses the glorious comfort that He had and that we have now:[34]

> O Lord, *You are* the portion of my inheritance and my cup;
> You maintain my lot.
> The lines have fallen to me in pleasant *places;*
> Yes, I have a good inheritance.
> I will bless the Lord who has given me counsel;
> My heart also instructs me in the night seasons.

---

[34] Peter specifically identifies that David prophetically wrote Christ's words in this song. Acts 2:25-35.

I have set the Lord always before me;
Because *He is* at my right hand I shall not be moved.
Therefore my heart is glad, and my glory rejoices;
My flesh also will rest in hope.
For You will not leave my soul in Sheol,
Nor will You allow Your Holy One to see corruption.
You will show me the path of life;
In Your presence *is* fullness of joy;
At Your right hand *are* pleasures forevermore.

Let us consider one expression of Christ's praise and comfort in
Psalm 31:19-24. Christ says,[35]

Oh, how great *is* Your goodness,
Which You have laid up for those who fear You,
Which You have prepared for those who trust in You
In the presence of the sons of men!
You shall hide them in the secret place of Your presence
From the plots of man;
You shall keep them secretly in a pavilion
From the strife of tongues.
Blessed *be* the Lord,
For He has shown me His marvelous kindness in a strong city!
For I said in my haste,
"I am cut off from before Your eyes";
Nevertheless You heard the voice of my supplications
When I cried out to You.
Oh, love the Lord, all you His saints!
For the Lord preserves the faithful,
And fully repays the proud person.
Be of good courage,
And He shall strengthen your heart,
All you who hope in the Lord.

√ *What lines of this song speak out to the comfort and assurances that
Christ had and we have?*

_____

_____

_____

[35] Christ directs us to this song as His words when He quoted from this song
from the cross. Luke 23:46.

Notice the victorious message in Psalm 20:6-9 where the victory of "His Anointed" is the source of our confidence.

> Now I know that the Lord saves His anointed;
> He will answer him from His holy heaven
> With the saving strength of His right hand.
> Some *trust* in chariots, and some in horses;
> But we will remember the name of the Lord our God.
> They have bowed down and fallen;
> But we have risen and stand upright.
> Save, Lord!
> May the King answer us when we call.

√ *What is the connection between God saving His Anointed and God saving us?*

Suffering plus Comfort leads to Praise. Praise for God is the consolation and comfort we have arising from sufferings and trials. It is not that Christ suffered. It is not that Christ was comforted. But the suffering and the comfort together have a purpose: to strengthen us and to cause us to praise Jehovah. As Paul said about the purpose of his suffering, it was so he would learn to trust God and not himself. "Yes, we had the sentence of death in ourselves, *that we should not trust in ourselves but in God who raises the dead,* who delivered us from so great a death, and does deliver us; in whom we trust that He will still deliver us..." 2 Corinthians 1:9-10. Throughout the Psalms, there is a balance of grief and consolation and praise. In most Psalms, grief and consolation are combined to peak in a crescendo of praise to God. This sequence of suffering, consolation and praise repeats throughout the Psalms. This is precisely what Paul spoke of when he said that we "exult in tribulation." Romans 5:3.This sequence must be realized in the lives of all of God's people.

Praise leads to proclamation! The beginning of Psalm 22 is often read with Isaiah 53 as insight to Christ's suffering. For denominations that take the Lord's Supper regularly, the first part of this song is often used as part of that sacrament. However, the conclusion of Psalm 22, verses 21-31, is a powerful progression of thoughts that leads to praise and ultimately spreading the good news to others:

You have answered Me.
I will declare Your name to My brethren;
In the midst of the assembly I will praise You.
You who fear the Lord, praise Him!
All you descendants of Jacob, glorify Him,
And fear Him, all you offspring of Israel!

For He has not despised nor abhorred the affliction of the afflicted;
Nor has He hidden His face from Him;
But when He cried to Him, He heard.
My praise *shall be* of You in the great assembly;
I will pay My vows before those who fear Him.
The poor shall eat and be satisfied;
Those who seek Him will praise the Lord.
Let your heart live forever!
All the ends of the world
Shall remember and turn to the Lord,
And all the families of the nations
Shall worship before You. For the kingdom *is* the Lord's,
And He rules over the nations.
All the prosperous of the earth
Shall eat and worship;
All those who go down to the dust
Shall bow before Him,
Even he who cannot keep himself alive.
A posterity shall serve Him.
It will be recounted of the Lord to the *next* generation,

They will come and declare His righteousness to a people who will be born,
That He has done *this.*

The pulpit has often criticized the pews saying that they are not evangelizing as they should. Common churchgoers are not spreading the gospel. However, if we realize God's work in our lives *and praise Him for it*, sharing the gospel would be a natural outgrowth of that praise.

✓ *What connection do you see between praise for God and our declaration to the world of His great deeds?*

✓ *Treasure hunt: Where are* you *mentioned in Psalm 22?*

Our comfort comes from God. Where do we find solace? Peter said,

> Grace and peace be multiplied to you in the knowledge of God and of Jesus our Lord, as His divine power has given to us all things that *pertain* to life and godliness, through the knowledge of Him who called us by glory and virtue, by which have been given to us exceedingly great and precious promises....

2 Peter 1:2-4. However, one person recently gave his opinion about the sufficiency of the scriptures:

> I would not know who Jesus is if it were not for books. I would know hardly anything about peace, justice, or love if it were not for books. Basically, knowing what I now know, I fear that I would be an incredibly depressed and hopeless person if it were not for books. When I say books, I am not talking about the Bible. I am talking about books about the Bible, and also books that have nothing to do directly with the Bible.[36]

The Apostle Peter and this man are in direct conflict with each other.

✓ *Are other books necessary for us to have an understanding of Christ's sufferings, His victory, and His comforting? Are man-written books— such as devotional books or books of common prayer—necessary for us to understand and receive the comfort He has for us as His people? How much reliance should we place on man-written thoughts?*

✓ *Sing Psalm 34 again which appears on the next page. If you are using this book with a group you may wish to sing the last section in bold to conserve time.*

---

[36] "The Bible Is Not Enough," Thinking, Reflecting, Seeking...Questioning, http://tamostul.wordpress.com/2012/02/19/the-bible-is-not-enough/, retrieved February 5, 2013.

Psalm 34

God will I bless all times; his praise
My mouth shall still express.
My soul shall boast in God: the meek
Shall hear with joyfulness.

Extol the Lord with me, let us
Exalt his name togeth'r.
I sought the Lord, he heard, and did
Me from all fears deliv'r.

They looked to him, and lightened
were:
Not shamed were their faces.
This poor man cried, God heard, and saved
Him from all his distress's.

The angel of the Lord encamps,
And round encompasseth
All those about that do him fear,
And them delivereth.

O taste and see that God is good:
Who trusts in him is blessed.
Fear God his saints: none that him fear
Shall be with want oppressed.

The lions young may hungry be,
And they may lack their food:
But they that truly seek the Lord
Shall not lack any good.

O children, hither do ye come,
And unto me give ear;
I shall you teach to understand
How ye the Lord should fear.

What man is he that life desires,
To see good would live long?
Thy lips refrain from speaking guile,
And from ill words thy tongue.

Depart from ill, do good, seek peace,
Pursue it earnestly.
God's eyes are on the just; his ears
Are open to their cry.

The face of God is set against
Those that do wickedly,
That he may quite out from the earth
Cut off their memory.

The righteous cry unto the Lord,
He unto them gives ear;
And they out of their troubles all
By him deliver'd are.

The Lord is ever nigh to them
That be of broken sp'rit;
To them he safety doth afford
That are in heart contrite.

The troubles that afflict the just
In number many be;
But yet at length out of them all
The Lord doth set him free.

He carefully his bones doth keep,
Whatever can befall;
That not so much as one of them
Can broken be at all.

Ill shall the wicked slay; laid waste
Shall be who hate the just.
The Lord redeems his servants' souls;
None perish that him trust.

This song may be sung to the tune of "Must Jesus Bear His Cross Alone," or to any of the following: "How Sweet, How Heavenly," "How Shall the Young Secure Their Hearts," "Jesus, the Very Thought of Thee," or "When All Thy Mercies."

10:LOVE
LETTERS

A married couple has private communications that others never see or hear. True soul-mates bare their souls and innermost thoughts with each other. Before electronic communication, cards and letters were sent between a husband and wife when they were apart. The love letters of historical soul-mates give windows into their being: their intimate expressions and personal concerns. Between some couples, the letters contain only expressions of love and praise. Sometimes, they express a longing to be reunited. Other times, the letters express frustration, anger or feelings of being unloved or ignored. But almost always, they end with an expression of love: "Very affectionately yours," "Your own loving and devoted," or "As ever your devoted and loving husband."[37]

There is a love relationship between God and us. The scriptures are full of factual statements of love of God for us and us for God: "For God so loved the world." "We love, because He first loved us." "Love the LORD your God with all your heart..." God frequently refers to the relationship between Himself and His people in marital terms: Ezekiel 16, Ephesians 5:22-32, 2 Corinthians 11:2, the entire book of Hosea, and Revelation 19:7. It is no wonder that the scriptures end in a crescendo with the preview of the marriage between Christ and His church: "Come, I will show you the bride, the Lamb's wife." Revelation 21:9.

The Praises are love letters. The Psalms are love letters between God and us. Sometimes the expressions are plain: "I love the LORD, because

---

[37] http://www.everydaycorrespondence.com/2009/11/valedictions-iii-historic-letter.html, retrieved January 29, 2013.

He has heard My voice...." Psalm 116:1. "The LORD loves the righteous." Psalm 146:8. But most of the other times, the Psalms express the idea of God's love for us in His care for us. Nearly all the Psalms express our love for God in the terms of praise for Him. It is no wonder that the Jews called this the Book of Praises or Hymns.

Shouting for Joy! Tom Cruise appeared on Oprah Winfrey's talk show and infamously jumped on her couch when he talked about his love for his then-fiancé (and now ex-wife), Katie Holmes. He couldn't contain his excitement.[38] That exuberant love, a jump-on-the-couch type of love, is what we should have for God. It is displayed in the Praises.

√ *Sing a Praise! Sing the Praise that appears on page 70. (If you are constrained by time, you may choose to sing only several verses of the song.)*

The last Praise in the Book of Psalms, Psalm 150, is brief and wonderful. Looking back to prior chapters, remember (1) musical instruments were only used by priests in connection with sacrifices and calls to worship, and (2) the Jews did not use musical instruments when they sang these songs, (3) *we* are now God's temple or sanctuary, and (4) the sanctuary and temple rituals are symbols of the spiritual acts and relationships we have under the New Testament.

> Praise the Lord!
> Praise God in His sanctuary;
> Praise Him in His mighty firmament!
> Praise Him for His mighty acts;
> Praise Him according to His excellent greatness!
> Praise Him with the sound of the trumpet;
> Praise Him with the lute and harp!
> Praise Him with the timbrel and dance;
> Praise Him with stringed instruments and flutes!
> Praise Him with loud cymbals;
> Praise Him with clashing cymbals!
> Let everything that has breath praise the Lord.
> Praise the Lord!

---

[38] "13 Shocking *Oprah Show* Moments," http://www.oprah.com/oprahshow/ The-Oprah-Shows-Most-Shocking-Moments_1/6, retrieved February 5, 2013.

If we forget that the Praises are using powerful symbols for us today, we may miss out on the power of God's Praises. Here are several questions to consider in singing this Praise.

✓ *Where is His sanctuary now? (verse 1)*

✓ *What does the Holy Spirit mean in verse 6 when He says, "Let everything that has breath praise the Lord"? Is that literal?*

✓ *What are the Lord's mighty acts? (Hint: for the Israelites, it would have been the delivery from Egypt, the crossing of the Red Sea, etc. For us see 1 Corinthians 10:1-4 for a clue.)*

✓ *Since this Psalm begins and ends with symbolism, what does the use of noisy, musical instruments symbolize?*

When we are liberated from taking this song literally, we can see the exuberance, the enthusiasm, and the ecstatic joy that *we* are to have for the LORD. We are to have so much love for God that we cannot contain ourselves! When is the last time you felt like that when you were singing? When we speak or sing about God, we should feel like jumping on the couch, so to speak. When is the last time you felt like that when you were praising God?

Bubbling over with Praise. Consider Praise 145 and the exuberance that the Holy Spirit places in our mouths:

> I will extol You, my God, O King,
> And I will bless Your name forever and ever.
> Every day I will bless You,
> And I will praise Your name forever and ever.
> Great is the LORD, and highly to be praised,

And His greatness is unsearchable.
One generation shall praise Your works to another,
And shall declare Your mighty acts.
On the glorious splendor of Your majesty
And on Your wonderful works, I will meditate.
Men shall speak of the power of Your awesome acts,
And I will tell of Your greatness.
They shall eagerly utter* the memory of Your abundant goodness
And will shout joyfully of Your righteousness.

literally "bubble over with"

✓ *Can you feel the enthusiasm this song conveys? If we all felt this way, what would the world know about God from our words and feelings?*

_____

_____

Sometimes we feel ignored and abandoned. God created us so He knows how we feel. Christ lived as a man with us so He knows how we feel. Just as in a marriage one spouse may feel ignored, God knew that we would feel that way, too, on occasion. He knows that we need to express those feelings of abandonment. One psychologist said, "No shrink would promote verbal or physical abuse in a relationship, but those worth their salt know that anger and its expression are part of the human condition and shouldn't always be suppressed. When they are over a long period of time, resentment and a lack of fulfillment result."[39] God has provided a way for us to vent and be angry with Him.

Assurances of His love and care. Each complaint vented in the Book of Praises is always followed by an assurance of God's love and care for us. God never leaves us feeling abandoned: He points out his faithfulness and power to support us. Then we pass it along to others. "I will make known Your faithfulness to all generations." Psalm 89.

✓ *Consider the "complaints" from the Psalms in the table in the next column. How do the assurances and praises "balance" or resolve the complaints?*

_____

_____

[39] Rob Dobrenski, Phd., "Why Marriages Fail." http://shrinktalk.net/?p=151, retrieved February 5, 2013.

Complaint	Assurance
Psalm 13	
How long, O Lord? Will You forget me forever? How long will You hide Your face from me? How long shall I take counsel in my soul, *Having* sorrow in my heart daily?	But I have trusted in Your mercy; My heart shall rejoice in Your salvation. I will sing to the Lord, Because He has dealt bountifully with me.
Psalm 10	
Why do You stand afar off, O Lord? *Why* do You hide in times of trouble?	The Lord *is* King forever and ever; The nations have perished out of His land. Lord, You have heard the desire of the humble; You will prepare their heart; You will cause Your ear to hear, To do justice to the fatherless and the oppressed, That the man of the earth may oppress no more.
Psalm 89	
How long, Lord? Will You hide Yourself forever? Will Your wrath burn like fire? Remember how short my time is; For what futility have You created all the children of men? What man can live and not see death? Can he deliver his life from the power of the grave?	I will sing of the mercies of the Lord forever; With my mouth will I make known Your faithfulness to all generations. For I have said, "Mercy shall be built up forever; Your faithfulness You shall establish in the very heavens."... And the heavens will praise Your wonders, O Lord; Your faithfulness also in the assembly of the saints. For who in the heavens can be compared to the Lord? *Who* among the sons of the mighty can be likened to the Lord? God is greatly to be feared in the assembly of the saints, And to be held in reverence by all *those* around Him. O Lord God of hosts, Who *is* mighty like You, O Lord? Your faithfulness also surrounds You.

God's love language. Not every person appreciates the same things in the same way. Not every person appreciates the same kind of expressions of love. Some people believe God wants just any type of expression, much the same way that a parent is appreciative of a kindergartener's Father's Day gifts made of popsicle sticks and glitter. Besides being a parent-child relationship, God's relationship with us is also described as a *marriage*–much deeper. One marriage counselor identified different "languages" for expressing love between a husband and wife.[40] Some relationships get into trouble when one person is expressing love in a way that has no meaning to the other spouse or is giving her something she absolutely does not want. So in a relationship, it is important to give the other person what he or she appreciates.

But what is God's "language" of love? What expressions of praise does God want us to give to Him? Is He happy with anything we throw his way? Popsicle sticks and glitter? For "who has known the mind of the Lord that he may instruct Him?" "For what man knows the things of a man except the spirit of the man which is in him? Even so no one knows the things of God except the Spirit of God." 1 Corinthians 2:16, 11. God has not left us ignorant of how He should be praised. Absolutely not. God has given us "all things pertaining to life and godliness." 2 Peter 1:2-4. The Spirit has given us the Book of Praises. *He* knows the mind of Christ and the mind of the Father. The Spirit knows what thoughts and expressions have *the most meaning to God.* We are not left to guess what pleases God. We are not left to devise a form of "praise" that only makes us feel better.

✓ *If you were trying to please your spouse, would you do things that you like to do or would you do things that he or she appreciates? Is it different with God? Why or why not?*

_____

_____

✓ *For further meditation: Married couples often begin to think alike–to be "one" in thought as well as many other ways. We learned in earlier chapters that we are to have "the mind of Christ," who is described as the Bridegroom. Many of the praises have a dual application: they are both the words of Christ and they are the words of his people. Paul said, "Now may the God who gives perseverance and encouragement grant you to be of the same mind with one another according to*

---

[40] *See* Gary D. Chapman, *The Five Love Languages: The Secret to Love that Lasts.*

Christ Jesus, so that with one accord you may with one voice glorify the God and Father of our Lord Jesus Christ." Romans 15:5-6. We have one mind according to–in harmony with–Christ; and then with our "same mind" we have one voice glorifying God. How can singing the songs inspired by the Spirit of Christ help us to have the "mind of Christ"?

✓ *Sing the Praise, Psalm 116, below again.*

Psalm 116

I love theLord, because my voice
And Prayers he did hear.
I, while I live, will call on him,
Who bowed to me his ear.

Of death the cords and sorrows did
About me compass round;
The pains of hell took hold on me,
I grief and trouble found.

Upon the name of God the Lord
I then did call, and say,
Deliver thou my soul, O Lord,
I do thee humbly pray.

God merciful and righteous is,
Yes, gracious is our Lord.
God saves the meek; I was brought low,
He did me help afford.

O you my soul, do you return
Unto your quiet rest;
For, largely, unto you, the Lord
His bounty has expressed.

For my afflicted soul, from death
Delivered was by Thee:
You did my mourning eyes from tears,
My feet from falling, free.

I in the land of those that live
Will walk the Lord before.
I did believe, and therefore spoke:
I was afflicted sore.

I said, when I was in my haste,
That all men liars be.
What shall I render to the Lord
For all his gifts to me?

I'll of salvation take the cup,
On God's name will I call:
I'll make my vows now to the Lord
Before his people all.

In God's sight dear is his saints' death
Your servant, Lord, am I;
Your servant, and your handmaid's son
My bands You did untie.

This song can be sung to the following tunes: "Must Jesus Bear His Cross Alone" or "How Sweet, How Heavenly," "How Shall the Young Secure Their Hearts," "Jesus, the Very Thought of Thee," or "When All Thy Mercies."

11:CHRIST'S MINISTRY IN THE PSALMS

Spiders build intricate webs in order to capture prey. The structures that they build are uniquely designed with different lengths of strands in different connections. Each strand or area of the web vibrates in a unique way. If an insect were to be trapped in a particular section of the web, the spider–even if located on the opposite side of the web–will go to the exact location of the prey based upon the frequency of the vibration.[41] It is an amazing demonstration of the genius of God's design in the natural world.

God's word is a web of cross-connections from the beginning in the Garden of Eden to the New Jerusalem in the Book of Revelation. If we are sensitive to the connections between the various parts of the scripture, we can "feel" the vibrations no matter where we may be studying. We may be reading in one of Paul's letters and recognize a reference to Exodus or one of the prophets. It should not be surprising that the Psalms reverberate in different sections of the New Testament generally, and in the teachings of Christ in particular.

Jesus starts His ministry. Jesus started in His hometown of Nazareth by reading from Isaiah 61 in the synagogue and saying that this was being fulfilled before them. Luke 4:16-22 (quoting Isaiah 61). What Isaiah wrote foretelling the ministry of the Messiah is also proclaimed in Psalm 146:5-10. Compare the two scriptures:

---

[41] Paul Fornia, Margaret Noble, and Tiana Stastny, "Spider Webs - Do They Exhibit a Natural Network?" http://amath.colorado.edu/cmsms/index.php?page=spider-webs---do-they-exhibit-a-natural-network., retrieved January 29, 2013.

What Jesus read and what He announced that He was going to do:	What God, through Jesus, has done and is doing now:
The Spirit of the Lord *is* upon Me, Because He has anointed Me To preach the gospel to *the* poor; He has sent Me to heal the brokenhearted, To proclaim liberty to *the* captives And recovery of sight to *the* blind, *To* set at liberty those who are oppressed; To proclaim the acceptable year of the Lord. Isaiah 61:5-10	Happy *is he* who *has* the God of Jacob for his help, Whose hope *is* in the Lord his God... Who executes justice for the oppressed, Who gives food to the hungry. The Lord gives freedom to the prisoners. The Lord opens *the eyes of* the blind; The Lord raises those who are bowed down; The Lord loves the righteous. Psalm 146:5-8

The Holy Spirit told of Christ's ministry and purpose in the Psalms, too. Notice the different way these two parallel passages are phrased. One was meant for Christ to read and the other was meant for us to sing. Isaiah speaks of Christ's mission or purpose. Psalm 146 speaks of God accomplishing Christ's mission—it is in a present and ongoing tense. Psalm 146 had real meaning once Christ fulfilled it and made it a song for us.

The "I am's" of Jesus. The threads of Christ's identity run throughout the scriptures. It's no wonder that His identity is also revealed in God's songbook. In the Book of John, Jesus identified Himself metaphorically as different things. The Holy Spirit used these same metaphors in the Book of Praises or Hymns.

I am the Bread of Life. Jesus identified Himself as "the Bread of Life" and as "the Bread that came down from Heaven." John 6:35-41. Jesus used the same phrase as did the Holy Spirit in Psalm 78: "the bread came down from heaven." The "bread of heaven" or "manna" was a symbol for Christ. He is the Bread that came down when God "opened the doors of heaven"[42] and Christ is the only one who can satisfy our hunger. Psalm 78:23-25. And when we sing Psalm 132, it has even more meaning:

> For the Lord has chosen Zion;
> He has desired *it* for His dwelling place:
> "This *is* My resting place forever;
> Here I will dwell, for I have desired it.

---

[42] See also Luke 3:21-22, when "the heaven was opened" at the baptism of Jesus.

I will abundantly bless her provision;
I will satisfy her poor with bread.
I will also clothe her priests with salvation,
And her saints shall shout aloud for joy.
                    Psalm 132:13-16.

✓ *What is Zion? Who are "her Priests"? Who are "her saints"? Who are "her poor"? What or who is the bread?*

I am the light of the world. In John 1:9, John refers to Christ as "the light of men": "There was the true light which, coming into the world, enlightens every man." John 1:4-9. The Holy Spirit makes many references to "the Light" in the Psalms. "In Your light we see light." Psalm 36:9. "God *is* the Lord, And He has given us light...." Psalm 118:27. "The LORD is my light and my salvation..." Psalm 27:1. But Jesus Himself said, "I am the light of the world; he who follows Me shall not walk in the darkness, but shall have the light of life." John 8:12. It is no wonder, that this phrase is used in Psalm 56:13: "For You have delivered my soul from death, indeed my feet from stumbling, so that I may walk before God in the light of life."

I am the Door. Jesus said, "I am the door; if anyone enters through Me, he will be saved..." John 10:7. The Holy Spirit uses this same metaphor in Psalm 118:20: "This is the gate of the Lord, Through which the righteous shall enter." Later when Jesus said that He is the "true, living Way," Christ emphasized that "No one comes to the Father except *through* Me." Just as we go *through* the door or the gate, we can only go to the Father through Christ.

I am the Good Shepherd. Jesus said this twice. John 10:11 and 14. The people of God are referred to as the sheep of God's pasture. Psalm 79:13, 95:7, and 100:3. Since God's people are His sheep, it follows that God is our Shepherd. The Holy Spirit refers to Christ as the Shepherd of Israel: "Give ear, O Shepherd of Israel, You who lead Joseph like a flock; You who dwell between the cherubim, shine forth!" Psalm 80:1 And of course, He is referred to as the Shepherd in Psalm 23: "The LORD is my Shepherd."

As the Shepherd who lays down His life for his sheep, Jesus is also the Shepherd who searches for the single lost sheep that has gone astray. Luke 15:4-6. We are the sheep that are lost and need to be found. We should not be surprised that this parable is from *our* point of view in the

Psalms: "I have gone astray like a lost sheep; Seek Your servant, For I do not forget Your commandments." Psalm 119:176.

I am the true, living way.[43] Jesus said that He is "the true, living way." John 14:6. But the "living way" or the "way of life" is not a new idea in the scriptures; however, here Jesus emphasized that *He* is the way. "No one comes to the Father except through Me." In a Messianic Psalm, David through the Holy Spirit says, "You will make known to us the path of life." In other words, "You will make known to us the way of life." Psalm 16:11.[44] This is consistent with other songs: "Teach me your way, O LORD." Psalm 27:11 and Psalm 86:11. Then, in Psalm 67:1-2, the Holy Spirit says, "God be merciful to us and bless us, *And* cause His face to shine upon us, That Your way may be known on earth, Your salvation among all nations." Do you remember from Chapter 1 about parallelism in Hebrew poetry? Here is an example: "Your way" is equivalent to "Your salvation." "I have chosen the way of truth." Psalm 119:30.

✓ *These are not all the "I am" statements of Jesus. Neither are these all the metaphorical names for Christ. Consider the scriptures above, the identities listed in Chapter 6, and your own knowledge of the scriptures. Can you think of other metaphors for Christ? Can you find those titles or ideas located in the thoughts of the Praises?*

The Samaritan woman at the well. Jesus refers to several principles that were introduced in the Psalms. He refers to the concepts using the same imagery that the Spirit used. First, Christ told the woman, "Whoever drinks of this water will thirst again, but whoever drinks of the water that I shall give him will never thirst. But the water that I shall give him will become in him a fountain of water springing up into everlasting life." John 4:13-14. Psalm 36 says, "How precious *is* Your lovingkindness, O God!...You give [the children of men] drink from the river of Your pleasures. For with You *is* the fountain of life...." Psalm 36:7-9. "Bless...the Lord from the fountain of Israel." Psalm 68:26.

---

[43] "A more correct translation of this passage, according to the proper Hebrew idiom, would be, *'I am the true and living way.'*" David Webb, "Portraits of Jesus: The Way, the Truth and the Life." http://www.searchingthescriptures.net/main_pages/articles/portraits_of_jesus/portraits_of_jesus_1.htm. Retrieved February 2, 2013.

[44] Paul says specifically that Jesus is being referred to in this Psalm. Acts 13:35.

After the woman left the well and the disciples returned to Him, Jesus commented on the "harvest" that was to come. Jesus said, "Behold, I say to you, lift up your eyes and look at the fields, for they are already white for harvest! And he who reaps receives wages, and gathers fruit for eternal life, that both he who sows and he who reaps may rejoice together." John 4:35-36. Jesus is speaking of evangelism and the spreading of the gospel: there is a reference back to Psalm 126:5-6. There the Holy Spirit said, "Those who sow in tears shall reap in joy. He who continually goes forth weeping, bearing seed for sowing, shall doubtless come again with rejoicing, bringing his sheaves *with him.*" From Christ's words we know that Psalm 126 is about evangelism.

Psalm 72 describes Christ as the king. The hymn also states:

> There will be an abundance of grain in the earth,
> On the top of the mountains;
> Its fruit shall wave like Lebanon;
> And *those* of the city shall flourish like grass of the earth.

√ *Seeing that Psalm 72 is describing Christ and His kingdom and seeing how Christ described "the harvest," what does He mean regarding "an abundance of grain" and that "those of the city" shall "flourish like grass of the earth"? Why is there grain on the mountain tops?*

√ *For further meditation: We see that since Christ is the King of Psalm 72, there is "an abundance of grain in the earth." Just how large is the harvest that Christ is talking about when He says, "The harvest truly is great, but the laborers are few; therefore pray the Lord of the harvest to send out laborers into His harvest." Luke 10:2.*

The calming of the sea. Jesus slept in the stern of the boat during a great storm. The disciples were terrified and called on Jesus to help them: "Lord, save us! We are perishing!" Jesus rebuked the wind and immediately calmed the waters. Then they asked themselves, "Who can this be, that even the winds and the sea obey Him?" Mark 4:35-41. Knowing Psalm 107:23-32, they "knew" the answer but could not comprehend the fact: Jesus is Deity. This song beautifully gives the "rest of the story" on what happened in Galilee. We see God acting in the beginning. We see God calming the storm: "Then they cry out to the Lord in their trouble, and He brings them out of their distresses. He calms the storm, so that its waves are still." Psalm 107:28-29. Then we see God being praised, something missing from the Gospel account. Psalm 107:31-32. The Holy Spirit even tells us the purpose of this miracle. "Whoever *is* wise will observe these *things,* And they will understand the lovingkindness [grace] of the Lord." Psalm 107:43.

✓ *From the account in the Praises, what new things do we learn about what happened when Jesus calmed the sea?*

I desire mercy and not a sacrifice. When Jesus answered the Pharisees who were attacking Him and His disciples, He answered them "But if you had known what *this* means, 'I desire mercy and not sacrifice,' you would not have condemned the guiltless." Matthew 12:7. In His answer, Christ quoted from Hosea 6:6: "For I desire mercy and not sacrifice, And the knowledge of God more than burnt offerings." Had the Pharisees understood the extent of God's mercy, they would not have been so quick to condemn. The term "mercy" appears 100 times in the Book of Psalms in the New King James Version. While some are pleas for mercy, many are descriptions of God's mercy:

All the paths of the LORD are mercy and truth. Psalm 25:10.

But You, O Lord, are a God...abundant in mercy and truth. Psalm 86:15.

For the LORD is good; His mercy is everlasting.... Psalm 100:5.

The LORD is merciful and gracious, Slow to anger, and abounding in mercy. Psalm 103:8.

The Pharisees should have known that there were things more important than sacrifices such as repentance and obedience. Consider Psalm 40:6-8:

Sacrifice and offering You did not desire...
Burnt offering and sin offering You did not require...
I delight to do Your will, O my God,
And Your law is within my heart."

And then consider Psalm 51:16-17:

For You do not desire sacrifice, or else I would give it;
You do not delight in burnt offering.
The sacrifices of God are a broken spirit,
A broken and a contrite heart—
These, O God, You will not despise.

If the Pharisees had understood the importance of mercy over their legalistic opinions, they would not have judged Christ's disciples so quickly. If they understood that God values a broken spirit who delights to do God's will, they might have realized their own shortcomings.

✓ *We are sometimes so quick to "cast stones" at the Pharisees for their attitudes that we don't see the "Pharisee" in ourselves. What application do these principles from the Psalms have for us today?*

God's word is a treasure. The concept of the things of God being treasures more valuable than anything else is a familiar concept in the Psalms. When the treasure is found, it is a cause for rejoicing and celebration. Jesus said, "Again, the kingdom of heaven is like treasure hidden in a field, which a man found and hid; and for joy over it he goes and sells all that he has and buys that field." Matthew 13:44. The value of God's commandments that lead to His kingdom—salvation—was a concept completely familiar to those Psalm-singing Jews. As children, they would have memorized these lines from Psalm 119: "I rejoice at Your word as one who finds great treasure." 119:162. "Therefore I love Your commandments more than gold, yes, than fine gold!" Psalm 119:127. "The law of Your mouth is better to me than thousands of coins of gold and silver." 119:72.

Being born of the water and the Spirit. When Jesus spoke to Nicodemus, He said, "Most assuredly, I say to you, unless one is born of water and the Spirit, he cannot enter the kingdom of God. That which is born of the flesh is flesh, and that which is born of the Spirit is spirit. Do not marvel that I said to you, 'You must be born again.'" John 3:5-7. Although being "born again" is not mentioned directly, the Holy Spirit hints at it in several of His hymns. In Psalm 51:10, David in the Spirit said, "Create in me a clean heart, O God, and renew a steadfast spirit within me." Here the Spirit speaks of "*creating*" and "*renewing*": the actions which occur when we are born again–born of the spirit. Paul uses similar terms in describing our salvation, "He saved us, through the washing of *regeneration* and *renewing* of the Holy Spirit...." Titus 3:5. Another hint comes in Psalm 87 where the Holy Spirit speaks of those who are "born in Zion." Since the only thing on the hill of Zion was the Temple, no person from the nation of Israel would have been actually born there. So how would a person be "born in Zion?" The only explanation is a spiritual one: when we are born of the Spirit, we are spiritual citizens of Zion, the dwelling place of God.

> And of Zion it will be said,
> "This one and that one were born in her;
> And the Most High Himself shall establish her."
> The Lord will record,
> When He registers the peoples:
> "This one was born there."

Paul refers to the saved–those who were born again–saying that their "names *are* in the Book of Life." Philippians 4:3. In Revelation 21:22-27, we see those are registered, those whose names are written in the Lamb's Book of Life, dwelling in God and the Lamb as their Temple, spiritual Zion: "But I saw no temple in it, for the Lord God Almighty and the Lamb are its temple... But there shall by no means enter it anything that defiles, or causes an abomination or a lie, but only those who are written in the Lamb's Book of Life."

More teachings than these. As set forth in the preface to this book, this book cannot be exhaustive. There is not room enough or time enough to speak of every point. So we can't discuss the many points in the Sermon on the Mount that are lifted directly from the Book of Psalms such as many of the "Beatitudes": for example "The humble will inherit the land." Psalm 37:11. Or when Jesus said, "Not what goes into the mouth defiles a man; but what comes out of the mouth, this defiles a man," He mirrors what the Holy Spirit said: "Set a guard, O Lord, over my mouth; Keep watch over the door of my lips." Matthew 15:11 and Psalm 141:3. Or when Jesus said, "I am the vine and the Father is the vine dresser," He echoes what was written in Psalm 80. As Christians become more familiar with the Book of Psalms, they will become more sensitive to the repetition of symbols and of messages that appear elsewhere in the scriptures, especially in the New Testament.

✓ *If a song or hymn from the Book of Psalms contains principles Jesus or the Apostles announced as and used as authority, what value would it be to sing that song or hymn today? Would you have to examine it closely to see if it taught error? Why or why not?*

_____

_____

✓ *Take time to sing the song below. Can you see Christ in the song?*

Psalm 62:5-8

> Yet, O my soul, upon the Lord
> Still patiently attend;
> My expectations and my hope
> On Him alone depend.
>
> He only my salvation is,
> And my strong rock is He;
> He only is my sure defense;
> And moved I shall not be.
>
> In God alone my glory is,
> And my salvation sure;
> My rock of strength is in the Lord,
> My refuge most secure.
>
> On Him, ye people, evermore
> With confidence reply;
> Before him pour ye out your heart;
> God is our refuge high.

This song can be sung to the following tunes: "How Sweet, How Heavenly," "How Shall the Young Secure Their Hearts," "Jesus, the Very Thought of Thee," "Must Jesus Bear the Cross Alone?" and "When All Thy Mercies."

12: THE SAME YESTERDAY TODAY AND FOREVER

Many people see a great break between the "God of the Old Testament" and the "God of the New Testament"–as though they were two separate beings. One atheist wrote, "The God of the Old Testament is arguably the most unpleasant character in all fiction: jealous and proud of it; a petty, unjust, unforgiving control-freak; a vindictive, bloodthirsty ethnic cleanser; a misogynistic, homophobic, racist, infanticidal, genocidal, filicidal, pestilential, megalomaniacal, sadomasochistic, capriciously malevolent bully."[45] C.S. Lewis's contempt for the Psalms mirrors this atheist's view in many ways: he called them "vulgar," "petty," "self-righteous," "contemptible" and "devilish."[46] Opinions like those of Lewis come from misreading the Psalms. For example, Psalm 137 ends with this line: "How blessed will be the one who seizes and dashes your little ones against the rock." On the surface, it appears shockingly cruel. In reality, it is not.

Our God is a God who never changes. "For I *am* the LORD, I do not change." Malachi 3:6. There are not two "Gods" in the scriptures. Just as the Lord does not change, Jesus does not change, either: "Jesus Christ is the same yesterday, today, and forever." Hebrews 13:8. Many people want to split God into two: an Old Testament God who is cruel and a New Testament God who is loving. But the same Spirit of God wrote both Testaments. If we see that some of the Psalms do not fit our image of God, then our image of God is wrong or our view of some of the Psalms is wrong or possibly both.

---

[45] Dawkins, Richard, *The God Delusion*, 51.

[46] Lewis, C.S., *Reflections on the Psalms* (Harcourt, 1958), 21-25.

Some of the songs in the Book of Psalms puzzle many people: a few seem unloving and condemning. Some people have called these puzzling psalms the "imprecatory" psalms. *Imprecate* is an obscure word that means to call down evil or curses on a person. "Imprecatory psalms" are those which call down curses on a person or group of people. Rather than use an obscure term, we'll call them "cursing songs" throughout this chapter. These songs seem to go against both the Old Testament ("You shall love your neighbor as yourself." Leviticus 19:18) and the New Testament ("And just as you want men to do to you, you also do to them likewise." Luke 6:31).

✓ *On the last page of this chapter is Psalm 12 which is sometimes called an "imprecatory psalm" or "cursing psalm." Take a moment to sing this song.*

Three categories: This chapter looks at these in three groups: (1) Songs that ask for vengeance, (2) Songs that are prophetic, and (3) Songs that just express things as they are.

Christians and the vengeance conundrum. If you remember we discussed in Chapter 3, there was only one song that was part of the Law of Moses. Moses wrote the lyrics down in Deuteronomy 32. One key phrase of this song (Deuteronomy 32:35) was repeated several times in the New Testament: "Vengeance is Mine; I will repay." Romans 12:19 and Hebrews 10:30. We know that we are to love our enemies and we are not to avenge ourselves. As Paul said, we need to "give place to wrath." Romans 12:19. How do we "give place to wrath? The Holy Spirit tells us, "Rest in the LORD and patiently wait for Him; Do not fret because of him who prospers in his way, because of the man who carries out wicked schemes. Cease from anger, and forsake wrath; Do not fret: it leads to evildoing." Psalm 37:7-9.

But is it wrong for us to ask God that His wrath be stirred up? Can we ask Him to avenge us of our enemies? Can *we* ask the Lord to rebuke our enemies? God's answers to these questions also come from the Holy Spirit's words. Throughout the Book of Praises are songs that contain just such requests. The Holy Spirit's words in the Book of Praises are completely in harmony with the New Testament. We know that the martyred saints asked God to avenge their blood: "How long, O Lord, holy and true, until You judge and avenge our blood on those who dwell on the earth?" Revelation 6:10. The Archangel Michael rebuked Satan saying, "May the Lord rebuke you." Jude 9. We know that Paul said, "Alexander the coppersmith did me much harm. May the Lord repay him according to his works." 2 Timothy 4:14. So yes, we can ask God to repay evildoers and avenge us when we are persecuted and suffer for His name. But we *never* should take God's work into our own hands.

The Path from Wrath to Peace. Rather than just blurting out a curse on our enemies, God's word shows us the path we should take so that we can leave a place for God's wrath. The Holy Spirit reveals a progression of thoughts we should have.

1. We are faced with a problem and express it to God.

2. We express our human "need" for justice against the evil ones causing our problems.

3. By the end of the song, a resolution is made that brings us to peace because of God's care and providence.

Psalm 83: Let's look at Psalm 83 as an example of such a "cursing song." For the sake of space, only the key verses are quoted.

Psalms 83		
The Problem	**Request for Vengeance**	**Resolution and Comfort**
Do not keep silent, O God! Do not hold Your peace, And do not be still, O God! For behold, Your enemies make a tumult; And those who hate You have lifted up their head. They have taken crafty counsel against Your people, And consulted together against Your sheltered ones. They have said, "Come, and let us cut them off from *being* a nation, That the name of Israel may be remembered no more." Psalm 83:1-4	O my God, make them like the whirling dust, Like the chaff before the wind! As the fire burns the woods, And as the flame sets the mountains on fire, So pursue them with Your tempest, And frighten them with Your storm. Psalm 83:13-15	Fill their faces with shame, That they may seek Your name, O Lord. Let them be confounded and dismayed forever; Yes, let them be put to shame and perish, That they may know that You, whose name alone *is* the Lord, *Are* the Most High over all the earth. Psalm 83:16-18

One point that makes this song so understandable to Christians is the *purpose* expressed for the punishment that is being requested: "That they may seek Your name" and "that they may know that you...are the Most High over all the earth." This is similar to what Paul said: "Deliver such a one to Satan for the destruction of the flesh, that his spirit may be saved in the day of the Lord Jesus." 1 Corinthians 5:5.

Psalm 5: Evil people have oppressed God's people for centuries. What happens to the oppressors? How do we ask God for help? Consider the last part of Psalm 5, which begins with a lament and ends in praise.

Psalm 5:8-12

The Problem	Request for Vengeance	Resolution and Comfort
Lead me, O Lord, in Your righteousness because of my enemies; Make Your way straight before my face. For *there is* no faithfulness in their mouth; Their inward part *is* destruction; Their throat *is* an open tomb; They flatter with their tongue.	Pronounce them guilty, O God! Let them fall by their own counsels; Cast them out in the multitude of their transgressions, For they have rebelled against You.	But let all those rejoice who put their trust in You; Let them ever shout for joy, because You defend them; Let those also who love Your name Be joyful in You. For You, O Lord, will bless the righteous; With favor You will surround him as *with* a shield.

Notice that this song asks for God to allow the wicked to fall by "their own counsels." In other words, their evil thoughts are to be their own undoing. This song asks that the oppressors of the righteous reap what they sow. It that so bad?

Psalm 58: Psalm 58 begins with the problem of evil men oppressing the righteous. Then it calls for vengeance. The song ends in consolation for the righteous and men acknowledge God as the judge of the earth.

Psalm 58		
The Problem	**Request for Vengeance**	**Resolution and Comfort**
Do you indeed speak righteousness, you silent ones? Do you judge uprightly, you sons of men? No, in heart you work wickedness; You weigh out the violence of your hands in the earth. The wicked are estranged from the womb; They go astray as soon as they are born, speaking lies. Their poison *is* like the poison of a serpent; *They are* like the deaf cobra *that* stops its ear, Which will not heed the voice of charmers, Charming ever so skillfully.	Break their teeth in their mouth, O God! Break out the fangs of the young lions, O Lord! Let them flow away as waters *which* run continually; *When* he bends *his* bow, Let his arrows be as if cut in pieces. *Let them be* like a snail which melts away as it goes, *Like* a stillborn child of a woman, that they may not see the sun. Before your pots can feel *the burning* thorns, He shall take them away as with a whirlwind, As in His living and burning wrath.	The righteous shall rejoice when he sees the vengeance; He shall wash his feet in the blood of the wicked, So that men will say, "Surely *there is* a reward for the righteous; Surely He is God who judges in the earth."

It is not unusual for people to be taken aback by the phrase "break their teeth." Notice the next line that clarifies it: "Break out the fangs of the young lions." The call to "break their teeth" or to "break their fangs" is to ask God to remove from them their means of hurting or oppressing the righteous. Then they will be as dangerous as a "toothless bulldog."

Some "curses" are prophesies. Many of the cursing songs have a deeper meaning and fulfillment than what may appear on the surface. If you will remember back to Chapter 8, Christ's words and thoughts are patterns for us to follow and place in our minds, particularly His thoughts of suffering. Some of these cursing songs are really windows into the mind of Christ. Consider the following songs: 35, 69 and 109.

Psalm 69: One of the most "infamous" of these cursing songs is Psalm 69. The most "notorious" section of the Psalm is in verses 22-28. But the song is not as "terrible" as it seems when we see it in context and compare it to the words of Christ.

First, to understand this passage, we need to understand who the speaker is. Paul identifies Christ as the speaker in Romans 15:3. The disciples recognized Christ as the subject of this Psalm: the phrase "Because zeal for Your house has eaten me up" is recognized as referring to Christ. John 2:17. It contains a prophecy about Christ that was fulfilled at the cross: "They also gave me gall for my food, and for my thirst they gave me vinegar to drink." Matthew 27:34, Mark 15:36, Luke 23:36 and John 19:30. The speaker is Christ.

Second, we need to understand who "they" are. "They" hated Christ without cause. Psalm 69:4. "They" gave Him gall and vinegar. Psalm 69:21. "They" are Christ's adversaries who persecuted, tortured and then crucified Him. "They" are the Jewish leaders. What did Christ say about them in other passages? Not surprisingly, He said the same things that are recorded in this Psalm.

✓ *The table below contains a passage from Psalm 69 and verses from Matthew 23. Do you see a connection between the "curses" of Psalm 69 and the "woes" pronounced by Christ?*

Psalm 69:22-28	Matthew 23
Let their table become a snare before them, And their well-being a trap.	Therefore you are witnesses against yourselves that you are sons of those who murdered the prophets. 31
Let their eyes be darkened, so that they do not see; And make their loins shake continually.	"Woe to you, blind guides...Fools and blind!...Fools and blind! 16-19
Pour out Your indignation upon them, And let Your wrathful anger take hold of them.	...that on you may come all the righteous blood shed on the earth, from the blood of righteous Abel to the blood of Zechariah, son of Berechiah, whom you murdered between the temple and the altar. Assuredly, I say to you, all these things will come upon this generation. 35-36
Let their dwelling place be desolate; Let no one live in their tents.	See! Your house is left to you desolate; 38

For they persecute the *ones* You have struck, And talk of the grief of those You have wounded.	Therefore, indeed, I send you prophets, wise men, and scribes: *some* of them you will kill and crucify, and *some* of them you will scourge in your synagogues and persecute from city to city... 34
Add iniquity to their iniquity, And let them not come into Your righteousness. Let them be blotted out of the book of the living, And not be written with the righteous.	Fill up, then, the measure of your fathers' *guilt*. Serpents, brood of vipers! How can you escape the condemnation of hell? 32-33

The phrase "Fill up, then, the measure of your father's guilt" sounds like a father's sins are being passed on to his sons. In reality, this phrase is quite prophetic. As co-high priests, Annas and his son-in-law Caiaphas were corrupt and enemies of Christ. They spearheaded the torture and death of Christ. Annas's sons continued in their father's ways and died horrific deaths.[47]

Psalm 35: This song has some harsh language for a certain group of people who "seek my life" and "plot my hurt." 35:4. But this Psalm is Messianic: "Fierce witnesses rise up; They ask me *things* that I do not know." 34:15.

> Let those be put to shame and brought to dishonor
> Who seek after my life;
> Let those be turned back and brought to confusion
> Who plot my hurt.
> Let them be like chaff before the wind,
> And let the angel of the Lord chase *them.*
> Let their way be dark and slippery,
> And let the angel of the Lord pursue them.
> For without cause they have hidden their net for me *in* a pit,
> *Which* they have dug without cause for my life.
> Let destruction come upon him unexpectedly,

---

[47] Annas was co-high priest with Caiaphas, his son-in law. Annas had two sons who followed in the family's corrupt behavior: Eleazar and Annas. The second Annas was responsible for the death of James. Eleazar led the revolt against Rome that lead to the destruction of Jerusalem. In a power struggle during the war with Rome, Annas was murdered by a rival faction. Eleazar then suffered through the siege. So, in this situation, there is a relation between the father's and the sons' guilt and punishment. Josephus, *The Jewish War,* 2.17.9 441.

And let his net that he has hidden catch himself;
Into that very destruction let him fall.

The works of Josephus, a Jewish historian, removes any doubt whether this type of destruction fell upon Jerusalem and, therefore, the Jewish leadership that persecuted Christ and His saints. It was horrific almost beyond description.

✓ *So what is Christ saying will happen to the Jewish leaders who persecuted Him and caused His suffering and death?*

_____

_____

Psalm 109: This song has been criticized for its harsh language. Its railing is against a single person: "Let there be none to extend mercy to *him*...Let *his* posterity be cut off...." Psalm 109:12-13. This song, however, was not a mystery to the Apostles. They recognized that this song referred to Judas. Acts 1:20. Jesus commented on Judas's consequences: "...but woe to that man by whom the Son of Man is betrayed! It would have been good for that man if he had never been born." Mark 14:21. We have the factual statement, but how did Jesus feel about Judas? The Holy Spirit tells us. When we read Psalm 109, we understand the gravity of what Jesus meant by "it would have been good for that man if he had never been born." Consider Psalm 109:6-20:

Set a wicked man over him,
And let an accuser stand at his right hand.
When he is judged, let him be found guilty,
And let his prayer become sin.
Let his days be few,
And let another take his office.
Let his children be fatherless,
And his wife a widow.
Let his children continually be vagabonds, and beg;
Let them seek their bread also from their desolate places.
Let the creditor seize all that he has,
And let strangers plunder his labor.
Let there be none to extend mercy to him,
Nor let there be any to favor his fatherless children.
Let his posterity be cut off,
And in the generation following let their name be blotted out.

Let the iniquity of his fathers be remembered before the Lord,
And let not the sin of his mother be blotted out.
Let them be continually before the Lord,
That He may cut off the memory of them from the earth;
Because he did not remember to show mercy,
But persecuted the poor and needy man,
That he might even slay the broken in heart.
As he loved cursing, so let it come to him;
As he did not delight in blessing, so let it be far from him.
As he clothed himself with cursing as with his garment,
So let it enter his body like water,
And like oil into his bones.
Let it be to him like the garment which covers him,
And for a belt with which he girds himself continually.
Let this be the Lord's reward to my accusers,
And to those who speak evil against my person.

The last verse switches from talking of one man and moves to plural. He gives a warning: "Let this be the Lord's reward to my accusers, and to those who speak evil against my person."

✓ *How will God treat those who speak evil of Christ? What does this mean for us today?*

_____

_____

Just saying things as they are. Many of the songs men list among the "cursing psalms," are really just statements of fact about what happens to evil people. For example, Psalm 6 says, "Depart from me, all you who do iniquity...All my enemies shall be ashamed and greatly dismayed; they shall turn back, they shall suddenly be ashamed." Psalm 6:8-10. Or Psalm 11:5-6: "The Lord tests the righteous, but the wicked and the one who loves violence His soul hates. Upon the wicked He will rain coals; Fire and brimstone and a burning wind shall be the portion of their cup." The Holy Spirit also says: "God shall likewise destroy you [the evil man] forever; He shall take you away, and pluck you out of your dwelling place, and uproot you from the land of the living." Psalm 52:5. When a Hymn declares how God will treat evil people, the Hymn is not a curse upon them. The Holy Spirit is merely stating facts.

Here's a puzzle that has stymied people for a long time. See if you can fit the pieces together. First, here are the pieces to the puzzle:

1. Babylon is a constant symbol for those who rebel against God and who practice evil constantly. In Revelation, the very name of Babylon is associated with "the Mother of Harlots and of the Abominations of the Earth." Revelation 17:5.

2. Babylon's "little ones" would be the offspring of Babylon–those who follow after Babylon in her sinful ways. This is similar to when Jesus said the Jewish leaders were "of your father the devil." God said that He would "cut off from Babylon...offspring and posterity." Isaiah 14:22.

3. Jesus said, "What then is this that is written:'The stone which the builders rejected Has become the chief cornerstone'? Whoever falls on that stone will be broken; but on whomever it falls, it will grind him to powder." Luke 20:17-18. Notice that "the stone" and "the rock" are always singular when it refers to Christ. Christ is going to judge all people. 2 Timothy 4:1

So, there are the pieces. Here is the puzzle:

> O daughter of Babylon, you devastated one,
> How blessed will be the one who repays you
> With the recompense with which you have repaid us.
> How blessed will be the one who seizes and dashes your little ones against the rock.

✓ *What is God saying in this Psalm? Who is the one who is blessed and who will repay all evil persons?*

_____

_____

✓ *If you are using this book as part of a group or class, take a moment to sing Psalm 12 again. After studying these "cursing songs," do you see this song differently as you sing it?*

_____

_____

Psalm 12

Help, Lord, because the godly man
Does daily fade away;
And from among the sons of men
The faithful do decay.

Unto his neighbor ev'ry one
Does utter vanity:
They with a double heart do speak,
And lips of flattery.

God shall cut off all flatt'ring lips,
Tongues that speak proudly thus,
We'll with our tongue prevail, our lips
Are ours: who's lord o'er us?

For poor oppress'd, and for the sighs
Of needy, rise will I,
Says God, and him in safety set
From such as him defy.

The words of God are words most pure;
They be like silver tried
In earthen furnace, seven times
That has been purified.

Lord, you shall them preserve and keep
Forever from this race.
On each side walk the wicked, when
Vile men are high in place.

This song may be sung to the tune of "I'm Not Ashamed to Own My Lord" or to any of the following: "How Sweet, How Heavenly," "How Shall the Young Secure Their Hearts," "Jesus, the Very Thought of Thee," "Must Jesus Bear the Cross Alone?," or "When All Thy Mercies."

TESTIMONIESAREWONDERFU
LTHEREFOREMYS
OULKEEPSTHEMK IN THEENTR
ANCEOFYOUR THE GWORDSGIV
ESLIGHTITGIVES EARLY UND
ERSTAND CHURCH INGTOTHES

13: PSALMS IN THE EARLY CHURCH

Every day for sixteen years, inmates ate breakfast, lunch and dinner at Rykers Island Prison in New York under a five foot by four foot painting of the crucifixion of Christ. The painting was dominated by a black splotch on a white cross. After many changes in prison administrators, no one knew who painted it, or how it even came to hang in the mess hall. If it was a decoration of a room for "forgotten" people, then the art was probably forgettable, too. Then, in 1981, someone looked at the painting's inscription: "For the dining room of the prisoners Rikers Island." And then there was the unmistakable signature of the painter: Salvador Dalì. It was worth $100,000.[48] Suddenly, a blotchy painting was appreciated for what it was and not disparaged for where it came from.

Similar to those hundreds of men who looked daily at the Dalì painting and viewed it as worthless, Christians today tend to disregard the Book of Praises because of where it comes from instead of valuing it for who its author is. Because the physical nation of Israel ceased to exist almost 2000 years ago, it would be easy to think that the Book of Praises or Book of Hymns is just a bunch of old decorations surrounding a forgotten people and a dead religion. However, the Christians of the first century had a completely different view.

The early church used the Praises to teach about Christ. Jesus said the Book of Psalms spoke about Him. "Then He said to them, 'These *are* the words which I spoke to you while I was still with you,

---

[48] "Valuable Dali Painting Found Hanging in Prison," *Tri City Herald*, March 24, 1981, p.10.

that all things must be fulfilled which were written in the Law of Moses and the Prophets and the Psalms concerning Me.' And He opened their understanding, that they might comprehend the Scriptures." Luke 24:44-45. Once Christ opened the minds of the Apostles so they could understand what was written in the Psalms concerning Him, the floodgates of explanation burst out in the scriptures.[49] After having learned from childhood the songs and the stories of their ancestors, their minds must have been racing, making connections to the law, prophecies and songs with what they had witnessed.

The Psalms in the Sermons. In the very first "gospel" sermon, Peter used the Book of Psalms, quoting Psalm 16, Psalm 132, and Psalm 110, to prove three key points: (1) Jesus was raised from the dead, (2) Jesus was seated on the throne of David, and (3) Jesus is both Lord and Christ. Acts 2:25-35. Peter, through the Holy Spirit, reminded the degenerate Jewish leaders of Psalm 118:22, the very same passage that Jesus Himself had quoted to them just before they murdered Him. Matthew 21:42 and Acts 4:11. Paul also turned to the Book of Praises when he preached in Antioch when he quoted from Psalm 2 and Psalm 16. See Acts 13:16-41.

The Hymns were used for Comfort. As we learned in previous chapters, the Hymns offered comfort to the Christians in the early church. After the Jewish leaders reprimanded Peter and John for speaking and teaching in the name of Jesus, they and their companions sang from Psalm 146 and Psalm 2. Acts 4. They received their comfort from the Book of Hymns. When Paul and Silas were imprisoned in Philipi, they were "praying and singing hymns of praise to God." Acts 16:25. A more literal translation would be that they "hymned" to God. The same word is used in Hebrews 2:12, "I will sing praise" which is a quote from Psalm 22:22. The Greek word used here is *humneo*, which refers to singing the Hymns from the Book of Praises, specifically the "Great Hallel," Psalms 113-118 and 136.[50]

---

[49] The writer acknowledges that the Law of Moses and Prophets are also mentioned here; however, those are not the subject of this study. However, Christ does refer to the Psalms as scripture.

[50] When the word *humneo* is used in Matthew 26:30 and Mark 14:26, it refers to singing the Great Hallel, or Psalms 113-118 and 136. "*Humneo*" would have the same meaning in these two instances, also. See, *Vine's Expository Dictionary of Old and New Testament Words* and *Thayer's Greek-English Lexicon of the New Testament* and *Smith's Bible Dictionary.*

✓ *A version of Praise 113, part of the Great Hallel, appears on page 97. If you are studying this book as part of a group, sing it now.*

✓ *How would singing Psalm 113, or a psalm like it, bring comfort to Paul and Silas?*

The Hymns were used for Teaching. By far the greatest use of the Praises was for teaching. Jesus and the writers of the New Testament used the Spirit's Songs as proof texts for a number of principles and facts. The songs actually teach New Testament principles. The chart below is a partial list of the principles that were proven through the Book of Praises.

Principle/Fact	New Testament	Praise
Jesus Christ is the Son of God.	Acts 13, Heb. 1	Psalm 2
Christ is superior to angels.	Hebrews 1	Psalms 45, 97, 102, 104 & 110
Christ would teach in parables.	Matthew 13	Psalm 78
All things are subject to Christ.	Hebrews 2	Psalm 8
Jesus Christ would be raised from the dead.	Acts 13	Psalm 16
Christ is the High Priest forever.	Hebrews 5-7	Psalm 110
Christ would sit on David's throne forever.	Acts 2	Psalms 89 and 132
All humanity is under sin.	Romans 3	Psalms 5, 10, 14, 36, & 140
Animal sacrifices do not take away sin.	Hebrews 10	Psalm 40
Righteousness does not come from works.	Romans 4	Psalm 32
Christ will repay us according to our deeds.	Matthew 16	Psalm 62
If we reject God, He will reject us.	Hebrews 3	Psalm 95
Constancy of God's love through persecution.	Romans 8	Psalm 44
Israel's rejection of Christ.	Romans 11	Psalm 69
Gentiles participate in God's mercy.	Romans 15	Psalm 18 and 117

Principle/Fact	New Testament	Praise
Christ considers us brethren.	Hebrews 2	Psalm 22
Our faith causes us to confess Christ to others.	2 Corinthians 4	Psalm 116
God has given Christians spiritual gifts.	Ephesians 4	Psalm 68
The wisdom of this world is foolishness.	1 Corinthians 3	Psalm 94
Be free from the love of money and trust only in God.	Hebrews 13	Psalm 118
Be harmonious and kindhearted.	1 Peter 3	Psalm 34
Be angry but do not sin.	Ephesians 4	Psalm 4

The early church sang the Psalms or Praises/Hymns. Just as the meanings of the Psalms exploded in the minds of the Apostles, they would have exploded in the minds of the early Christians, most of whom were from a Jewish background. The power of Peter's sermon on the day of Pentecost is lost on us because the Psalms are not imbedded in our minds today as they were imbedded in the minds of that audience. From the scriptures we know that they sang from the Book of Psalms or Praises. James told the early church to sing them when they were cheerful. "Is anyone cheerful? Let him sing psalms." If we had the verb "to psalm" in English, this phrase would be translated, "Let him psalm." James 5:13. The Christians in Jerusalem "lifted their voices to God with one accord" singing from Psalms 2 and 146. Acts 4:24-25. Paul and Silas probably sang Psalms to God while in jail.[51] Acts 16:25. "And at midnight Paul and Silas praying, were singing hymns to God...."[52] Referring to singing Psalms, Paul said, "I will sing [psalms] with

---

[51] "There is no means of knowing the genre of the hymns which Paul and Silas sang in the Philippian jail, but if we are correct in reasoning that the human spirit, under duress and trial, turns instinctively to what is familiar and well-known, there is then nothing to deny that the Psalms of the Old Testament ran through the dark prison, greatly to the interest of the missionaries' fellow-captives." Ralph P. Martin, *Worship in the Early Church*, p. 43.

[52] This quote is from Young's Literal Translation. Praying and "hymning" are both used together here without a conjunction indicating that the praying and praising are one act. It was not an uncommon practice for Christians to alternate singing a Psalm followed by a period of silent prayer. Paul Bradshaw, *Early Christian Worship*, p. 73-74.

the spirit, and I will also sing [psalms] with the understanding."[53] 1 Corinthians 14:15. Some scholars believe that the antiphonal psalm-singing practice–where a group is divided and sings back and forth to each other–is referred to in Ephesians 5:18-19. "...but be filled with the Spirit, *speaking to one another* in psalms and hymns and spiritual songs...."[54] Beyond this, Paul directs one church to use the singing of Psalms as part of their teaching. Colossians 3. The scriptures are clear that the singing of the Spirit's Songs from the Book of Psalms or the Book of Hymns was an established practice in the early church.

√ *Because the early church used the Book of Psalms to teach in song and to praise God in song, is it appropriate for the church in the twenty-first century to do these things, too? Why or why not?*

History shows Christians sang the Spirit's songs for centuries. We know from history that early Christians were very attached to the Psalms by their reactions to those who tried to introduce uninspired songs. The Gnostics, Arians, and other heretical sects, started writing their own "psalms." They "drew on the persuasive powers of music to spread their own religious tenets."[55] For about four centuries, the church battled to keep man-written songs out of the collective worship:

All songs contrary to the essence of Jewish tradition were branded heretical by the early Church fathers, at least one of who, Paul of Samosata, "abolished (in his congregation) the singing of hymns...which had been written recently by composers of the day," and reinstituted the ancient Hebrew usage. Athanasius (c. A.D. 298-373), while Bishop of Alexandria, disapproved of the "exquisite heretical songs," and his contemporary, Epiphanius, condemned "the heretic psalms...which do not conform to the ancient (i.e., Jewish) tradition."[56]

---

[53] The verb here in Greek is "to psalm" or sing a psalm(s). If "to psalm" was a verb in English, this would read: "I will psalm with the spirit, and I will also psalm with the understanding."

[54] Alfred Sendrey and Mildred Norton, *David's Harp*, p. 251.

[55] *Ibid*, p. 253.

[56] *Ibid*, p. 257.

Even as late as the fifth century it was said, "Davidic psalms are sung everywhere in the Church with all piety."[57]

Forgetting the Masterpieces. About the time the Emperor Constantine reorganized and "legitimized" Christian worship, man-written hymns started to become accepted, first by Pope Damasus I, who wrote some of his own hymns.[58] The ripple turned into a wave, and man-written songs were used in worship thereafter. Not even the reforms of Pope Gregory could reverse the tide for long: he commanded that only Psalms be sung or chanted without musical accompaniment.[59] This type of Psalm singing became known as "Gregorian chants." By the time of the Renaissance, the use of the Psalms in worship had vanished for all practical purposes. There was a slight revival by reformers, beginning with John Calvin publishing the *First Psalter* in 1539 and a complete version of the Psalms in 1562. Because North America was populated primarily by Protestants, immigrants escaping religious persecution, psalm singing prevailed on this continent until about the year 1800.[60] A worship war of sorts arose then between those congregations who wanted to sing scripture and those who preferred man-written songs. In most churches today, popular thoughts have won out over God's songs.

Masterpieces. There are many old masterpieces of song penned by the greatest mind that ever has existed or will exist–our God. Imagine just discovering these masterpieces as they did that valuable painting on a prison wall.

✓ *Sing Psalm 113, on the next page, as a forgotten masterpiece that our brothers and sisters treasured so many years ago.*

---

[57] *Ibid.*

[58] *Ibid.*, p. 254.

[59] Pope Gregory reintroduced the use of the inspired Psalms only without musical accompaniment in 590. The "Gregorian Chant," chanting the Psalms in Latin, remained a practice for the clergy for some centuries. Ironically, most common worshippers did not speak Latin. So despite their use, the Psalms had no meaning to them.

[60] Hamilton C. MacDougall, *Early New England Psalmody*, pp. 7-8.

Psalm 113

Praise God, ye servants of the Lord,
Praise, praise his name with one accord;
Bless ye the Lord, His name adore
From this time forth forevermore.

From rising unto setting sun,
Praised be the Lord, the mighty one.
O'er nations all God reigns supreme,
Above the heavens His glories beam.

O who is like the Lord our God,
Who makes the heavens His abode;
Who stoops to see from His high throne
What things in heaven and earth are done.

From dust He makes the poor to rise,
The needy who in dunghill lies;
That He with princes may him place,
With princes of his chosen race.

He gives the barren woman joy,
In keeping house, she finds employ.
And children joy to her afford.
Praise ye Jehovah; praise the Lord.

*This song can be sung to the tune of "From Every Stormy Wind that
Blows" "Jesus, we Just Want to Thank You." "Just as I Am," "O Master,
Let Me Walk with Thee," "Son of My Soul," "Sweet Beulah Land" "'Tis
Midnight, and on Olive's Brow" and "When I Survey the Wondrous
Cross."*

AFTERWARD

Because God's Inspired Songs are scarcely included in modern hymnals, one might think it difficult to start singing Psalms. It is not. Resources exist. It might take a little work. But the little work will yield great results.

The Reformed Presbyterian Church of North America is a conservative denomination that believes in a cappella singing of Psalms only. They have several collections of the Psalms that are quite easy to sing and are usually very faithful to the scriptures. Their *The Book of Psalms for Worship* was released in 2009 which is a revision of *The Book of Psalms for Singing*. Both books are distributed through Crown and Covenant Publications. The books contain all 150 psalms and multiple versions of many of the psalms. They also have a website, psalter.org, which has excellent resources.

Old material may be free if the copyrights have expired. Many are available on the internet: you will be limited only by your printer and pocketbook. The *1650 Scottish Metrical Version of the Psalms* is a translation of the Psalms into English verse and is said to be a more accurate transaltion than the King James version. If you are comfortable with the language of that era, then this might be a good choice for you. Slightly more modern is the *The Psalter: The Scottish Version of the Psalms Revised and the New Versions Adopted* published in 1872. The langauge is still slightly archaic. It is available through Google Books.

For good listening, the site thepsalmssung.org has a capella versions of songs from many of the previously mentioned sources. They are available at no cost. Also, an Australian group, The Sons of Korah, has very modern versions of the Psalms sung with instrumental accompaniment. The songs are very accurate to the scriptures and in several places are more accurate than some modern translations. Their songs are available through many christian book stores and through iTunes.

Beware of any "psalm" written by Isaac Watts. He detested the Psalms and wrote his songs so they would fool unwary worshippers into thinking they were singing scripture. Watts titled his first collection of songs *The Psalms of David, imitated in the language of the New Testament, and applied to the Christian state and worship.* Most people didn't get past the first four words of the title. At a time when most churches sang Psalms exclusively, Watts wrote them this way so that he could–as he said–get his songs "through the church door." His deceptions continue through today: not long ago an elder and an expert on hymns led in a worship service Watts's "The Lord My Shepherd Is" believing it to be inspired scripture, which it most definitely is not. It is too easy to become a Watts victim even today.

Many groups promote their own personal views and theologies and often alter the scriptures accordingly. They may be unaware that they are doing this. Unfortunately, rather than simply translating the scriptures, a slight twist ends up in some versions of the Psalms. Be vigilant to avoid man-written creeds and their sublte changes.

Many more resources will become available through the years with the Lord's help. Hopefully, you shall seek them out and allow God's songs to be imprinted on your heart.

TM

Bibliography

Bradshaw, Paul F. Early Christian Worship: A Basic Introduction to Ideas and Practice. Collegeville, MN: Liturgical, 1996. Print.

Davies, Philip R., and J. W. Rogerson. *The Old Testament World.* Louisville, KY: Westminster John Knox, 2005. Print.

Green, Jay P. The Interlinear Bible: With Strong's Concordance Numbers above Each Word. [s.l.]: Hendrickson, 1986. Print.

Kidner, Derek. *Psalms 1-72: An Introduction and Commentary on Books I and II of the Psalms.* London: Inter-Varsity, 1973. Print.

LeFebvre, Michael. *Singing the Songs of Jesus: Revisiting the Psalms.* Fearn, Ross-shire: Christian Focus Publications, 2010. Print.

Leslie, Elmer A. *The Psalms: Translated and Interpreted in the Light of Hebrew Life and Worship.* New York: Abingdon-Cokesbury, 1949. Print.

Macdougall, H. C. Early New England Psalmody; an Historical Appreciation, 1620-1820,. Brattleboro: Stephen Daye, 1940. Print.

Martin, Ralph P. *Worship in the Early Church.* Grand Rapids: Eerdmans, 1974. Print.

Mays, James Luther. Psalms: Interpretation - a Bible Commentary for Teaching and Preaching. Louisville: John Knox, 1994. Print.

Reardon, Patrick Henry. *Christ in the Psalms.* Ben Lomond, CA: Conciliar, 2000. Print.

Robertson, R. B., John Gailey, and United Presbyterian Church of North America. *The Psalter: The Scottish Version of the Psalms Revised and the New Versions Adopted by the United Presbyterian Church of North America, with Music.* United Presbyterian Board of Publication, 1872. Print.

Scroggie, W. Graham. *The Psalms: Psalms I to CL.* Westwood, NJ: Fleming H. Revell, 1965. Print.

Sendrey, Alfred, and Mildred Norton. *David's Harp; the Story of Music in Biblical times.* [New York]: New American Library, 1964. Print.

Vine, W. E. Vine's Expository Dictionary of Old & New Testament Words. Nashville, TN: T. Nelson, 1997. Print.

Viola, Frank. *From Eternity to Here: Rediscovering the Ageless Purpose of God.* Colorado Springs, CO: David C. Cook, 2009. 150+. Print.

Wilson, Jeff. "Introducing the Psalms." *Studies in the Psalms.* Temple Terrace, Florida: Florida College Book Store, 2007. 39-65. Print.

ABOUT THE AUTHOR

Originally from Phoenix Arizona, Tom Mann lives in Temple Terrace, Florida with his wife of over 30 years, Meladie Walker Mann. Tom has two children. He has a Bachelor's degree in Education, a Master's degree in English and a Doctorate in Law. He is a teacher, a lawyer and a mediator. He has taught English and Law to youth and adults at all levels, from junior high school to postgraduate levels. Currently, Tom has a mediation practice in the Tampa Bay area.

www.ingramcontent.com/pod-product-compliance
Lightning Source LLC
Chambersburg PA
CBHW070641030426
42337CB00020B/4107